The Power of E.Q.:
Social Intelligence, Reading People, and How to Navigate Any Situation

By Patrick King
Social Interaction and Conversation Coach at
www.PatrickKingConsulting.com

Table of Contents

CHAPTER 1: CULTIVATING CONVERSATIONAL INTELLIGENCE — 7

- EMPATHIC LISTENING AND RESPONDING — 9
- ACTIVE CONSTRUCTIVE RESPONDING — 19
- SHIFT RESPONSES VERSUS SUPPORT RESPONSES — 29

CHAPTER 2: PERSPECTIVE AS THE FOUNDATION OF EMPATHY — 45

- WHICH PERCEPTUAL POSITION ARE YOU IN? — 45
- PERSPECTIVE-TAKING—HOW TO BE MENTALLY FLEXIBLE — 54
- HANDLING BIG EGOS—INCLUDING YOUR OWN — 66

CHAPTER 3: TAKING CHARGE OF YOUR META-LANGUAGE — 81

- MINDFUL NONVERBAL COMMUNICATION — 81
- THE ART OF COLD READING — 95
- AVOID EMOTIONAL DISCONNECTORS AND "WORD TRASH" — 107

CHAPTER 4: BECOMING EMOTIONALLY INTELLIGENT — 127

THE EMOTIONS WHEEL AND LEARNING TO LABEL — 128
THE POWER OF EMOTIONAL VALIDATION — 141
HIGH-QUALITY QUESTIONING — 153

CHAPTER 5: OWN YOUR LIMITS — 169

HOW TO CREATE HEALTHY BOUNDARIES — 170
USE DEARMAN FOR POLITE REQUESTS AND REFUSALS — 180
THE PERFECT APOLOGY — 191

SUMMARY GUIDE — 207

Chapter 1: Cultivating Conversational Intelligence

Most of us like to think that we are good people, that we are kind, intelligent and attentive. However, despite the best of intentions, few of us are genuinely good communicators, and it's a rare person who never finds themselves misunderstood, alienated, or even in full-blown conflict. **This book is about developing the skills and insights needed to be one of those rare few who are experts at dialogue, emotions, and empathy.**

That said, the emotional intelligence we'll be discussing in this book is not some quiet, private thing that you develop purely for your own use—in that sense, it is not really "personal development." Rather, we will see that emotional intelligence is about how you develop yourself in relation to others.

In just the same way as general intelligence makes itself manifest in the world through accomplishment, creativity, learning, or understanding, emotional intelligence is also something we **do**, rather than something we **are**. And the primary way that we express and develop our emotional intelligence is with other people. In the chapters that follow we'll look at how emotional intelligence helps us listen to others, consider their perspectives, "read" their verbal and nonverbal expressions, ask questions, identify a wide range of subtle emotions, put boundaries in place without breaking rapport, and speak with clarity, conviction, and compassion.

When developing emotional regulation, self-awareness, and masterful communication skills, every person we encounter becomes our teacher, and every interaction becomes a chance to learn and grow as an emotionally intelligent social being. Let's dive in and begin at the most natural starting point: learning how to listen.

Empathic Listening and Responding

We live in a noisy, distracted world where everyone is trying to make themselves heard.

Empathic listening is sadly underdeveloped. This is the kind of listening that puts **total, genuine attention on the other person and the message they are trying to convey**. If we're honest, many of us try to merely give the impression of paying attention to someone, or play the role of a good listener without really being one. Can you think of the last time you sat in someone's presence and gave them your full attention?

It takes effort not to constantly think of what you'll say next, not to interrupt, not to rush in with your own opinions, experiences, arguments, perceptions . . . Not only does it take effort, but it comes with a certain degree of risk. It may seem counterintuitive, but authentic listening opens up a space of vulnerability—for the listener, too!

Setting aside your own point of view and your own idea of where the conversation should go is an act of faith and a show of goodwill to the other person. The modern world does not encourage the kind of receptivity that makes us great conversationalists. If we're honest, most of us would prefer not to do the work and rather focus on controlling the conversation, expressing ourselves, or making some point or other.

To be emotionally intelligent listeners, we need to go against the grain and make the effort required to set aside our own egos and become genuinely curious about someone else's world. Here are a few key principles to keep in mind.

Principle 1: Listen to understand, not to respond

The next time you're in a conversation with someone, notice your own thoughts and where they go when the other person is talking. Are you busily imagining all the things you're going to say when they stop speaking? Are you quietly formulating a counterargument or thinking of ways to steer the topic back to yourself or what you know?

When we are occupying this reactive state, we are not really doing justice to what we are being told. We are looking at the other person and their message as something to push off against or manipulate to our own ends. We are tempted to be always in a responding mode, barging in with our own thoughts and feelings and our interpretations of what the other person is trying to share.

Listening to understand is a completely different position to take. You are not reactive, but receptive—you are listening with the unspoken intention to truly absorb and comprehend what you're told. It's a state of being open and curious and genuinely wanting to grasp the *message*. Yet how many of us are quick to gloss over this message because we're in a hurry to quickly decide on our *opinion of the message*? As Stephen Covey says, "Seek first to understand, then to be understood." It's subtle, but it makes all the difference in the world.

Principle 2: Listen to *everything*

The "message" is made up of many components, the spoken words being just a small part. Communication is made of verbal and nonverbal information, so expand your perception to take in both. This takes a degree of attention, awareness, and focus perception. Facial expression, quality of voice, posture, gestures, what people are wearing, and the style of language they are using. Listen, even, to what *isn't* being said. We'll be looking more closely at this "meta-language" in a later chapter.

Principle 3: Don't conflate your experience with theirs

Good conversations are dynamic, and they flow and change, often with both partners' positions slightly altered by the end of the conversation. However, that's not the same as being careless and unaware of times when you might be tempted to see your own thoughts and feelings in the place of the other person's. Let's say a friend is telling you about their recent health scare. They are trying to share the general message, "I was terrified, and now I have a renewed appreciation for my health!"

But as you hear them speak, let's imagine you can't help filtering all that information through your own pet theories and opinions about doctors or the state of healthcare in your country. You (perhaps unconsciously) interpret what they say in terms of what you already think, picking out all the ideas that confirm your pre-existing perspective. Perhaps you respond by going on a mini rant about how difficult it is to receive good treatment these days, or jumping in with an anecdote about your own recent experiences with doctors. Meanwhile your friend, who was intending to take the conversation in quite a different direction ("Isn't good health precious? I've been given a new lease on life!") feels like you haven't really listened, and in response doesn't feel like listening to you as you ramble on ...

Principle 4: Empathic listening takes effort—but not as much effort as correcting misunderstandings!

Throughout this book you may be struck by just how much work it takes to establish clear, compassionate lines of communication with another person. You might wonder whether all this is really worth it—the answer is yes! That's because the alternative is actually a lot more work in the long run. If you're a poor communicator, you pay for it by feeling disconnected and alienated from others, or worse, you find yourself frequently misunderstood or in conflict with them. Constantly missing people or never quite feeling that you're on the same wavelength is like poison for any relationship—and it takes incredible amounts of effort to make things right again.

Principles of emotionally intelligent, mindful, and empathetic communication exist for a reason: because they really are the easiest and most effective way of doing things. The better you become at these skills, however, the more you will see the incredible freedom they give you, and the deeper, richer kinds of relationships they allow you to have with others. Luckily for all of us, these skills can be acquired and developed.

<u>The Four Types of Empathic Responses</u>

Be honest: When someone says, "I know how you feel," does it make you feel any better? Probably not!

But then, what *should* you say? While you work on your emotional intelligence skills, here are a few easy responses that keep you in the receptive, understanding mode and let the other person know you're listening. These responses are also a great way to "buy time" and keep the conversation going when you're unsure of how to respond but want to show compassion anyway.

Type 1: Acknowledging their courage

If someone is sharing something vulnerable with you, or conveying an emotional message, it can be difficult to know what to say. But relax—you don't have to solve their problems or suddenly dispense sagely advice. One of the most powerful things you can do is simply acknowledge how challenging it is to merely speak up about such things.

"Thank you for sharing that with me. It means a lot."

"I know it's not easy to talk about these things, so I applaud you for that."
"You've done a good thing by speaking out."

Acknowledge the effort, bravery, and vulnerability it takes to share something personal. Just remember to keep things positive by focusing on strengths, resources, and achievements. A common empathetic response is to point out their strength of character:

"Wow, that couldn't have been easy, but you handled the situation with a lot of patience and tact."

Type 2: Clarifying the message

Pulitzer Prize-winning oral historian Studs Terkel tells us, "Don't be an examiner, be the interested inquirer." If you're ever stumped for what to say, ask a question. This alone will show that you are paying attention and value what the other person has to say—even better if you can ask a thoughtful question that shows you have been listening carefully. The right questions can help you understand the message, to confirm you've understood, and to quietly reassure the speaker that you respect and care about what they're saying and want to understand it correctly.

"So it seems like it was a really confusing few years. Have I got that right?"
"You were a student nurse at the time, weren't you?"
"Just so I can understand, are you saying you felt embarrassed when he said that? Or was it more that you were annoyed?"

Type 3: Conveying that you care

Much of the time, people share grievances or express their emotions not because they want someone to solve their problems for them or come up with a clever-sounding interpretation. Instead, we're often (sometimes unconsciously) looking for someone to validate and confirm what we're feeling, to listen, and to treat our experience as worthy of attention and concern.

Truly showing that you care in this way can be far more powerful than giving "good advice" or having some sagely council to offer. Think about a time in your life when you needed to speak to someone and remind yourself of the kind of response that would have most assured you. Most likely, you would have wanted the message: "I see you, and I hear you. I get it. It makes sense that you feel this way. People care about you and you matter." In fact, a demonstration of care without adding in some advice or a solution can feel the most empathetic of all:

"I'm here for you. Would you like to talk?"
"Is there anything you'd like me to help you with?"
"I care about you/this."

Type 4: Checking in

Show other people that you are attentive to their experiences and are paying attention to them. Deliberately check in to show that you care about how they're doing, and keep those lines of communication open. Even if someone doesn't respond fully to your checking in, they will still register that you cared enough to do so, and that's worth a lot.

"How are you feeling today?"

"Hey, how did things pan out with your neighbor?"
"You seemed a little unhappy in the meeting today. Are you okay?"

Keep such questions open-ended and genuinely listen to whatever you're told. If you can demonstrate to people that you've heard what they've said in previous conversations and remembered the core emotional details, you will send them the strong message that you are an active, engaged listener.

Active Constructive Responding

Being fully present and responding with any of the above empathetic responses will take you far. But let's carry things a little further. Here we'll look at what's called "active constructive communication." The idea was coined by Gable et al. in 2004, in an interesting research paper titled "What do you do when things go right? The intrapersonal and interpersonal benefits of sharing positive events."

The researchers were interested in the way that people respond to others in communication, specifically how they respond to being told about experiences, thoughts, and personal feelings. It's one of those small things that makes an enormous difference.

Imagine someone tells their friend excitedly that they've just won an award. The friend says, "Oh, cool. By the way did I tell you what I saw at the grocery store this morning?"

Looking at this exchange, you can easily see how the person might feel completely cut off, snubbed, or dismissed. The friend has shared some emotional content ("I'm proud of myself! I'm excited!"), and the friend has responded to this sharing of the self with a complete lack of tact or synchrony. In giving this response, the friend has put himself *at odds* with the speaker—they are no longer conversing together in sync, but communicating against one another ("I'm not especially proud of you. I'm bored, I don't care, what's next?").

This little exchange might not register to anyone as violent or abusive, but it is *destructive*. If such a lack of synchrony continues in this friendship, you can expect a breakdown of goodwill over time, misunderstandings, anxiety, conflicts, hurt feelings, and vague negativity that is difficult to put a finger on.

Constructive conversation, on the other hand, is different. It is courteous, warm, and based around positive feelings of accord, rapport, and harmony. It's like a state of flow where both parties feel heard and understood, and like conversations move in unison rather than out of sync. Constructive conversations tend to deepen relationships over time as they increase trust and coherence.

In the previous section we saw how important it is to have empathy for people who are in distress. But it's just as important to pay attention to how we respond to people when they are happy or are expressing themselves neutrally. In fact, there is some evidence that **our response to someone's positive expressions is a bigger determinant of the relationship quality than how we treat them when they're unhappy** (Gable, Gonzaga, & Strachman, 2006).

We can imagine that our responses to a message can vary according to whether they are active or passive, and whether they are constructive or destructive, as described above. This gives us four potential types of response:

- Active and constructive
- Passive and constructive
- Active and destructive
- Passive and destructive

Let's return to our earlier example to show how these different responses may play out in real life.

Person A says to Person B, in a loud and excitable voice, with a huge grin on their face, "You'll never guess what! You know that student film I made a few years ago? The one I submitted to that competition? Well, I won an award for it! I can't believe it!"

Looking at the tone of voice, body language, and verbal expression, it's not hard to see that Person A is excited, proud, and pleasantly surprised. It's also not too difficult to imagine what kind of response they'd most like. The very fact that Person A is telling Person B in the first place is sending the obvious message: "This news is important to me. I wanted to share it with you. Are you proud of me too?"

Now imagine that Person B was busy on their phone, doing something else when this message was delivered. There are a few ways to respond:

Active Constructive Response
Person B puts their phone away, stands up, and gives Person A an enormous hug, smiling as they do so and saying, "Oh my God, really? That's amazing! Look at you, you're like this fancy filmmaker now!"

This response matches the energy and enthusiasm of the message being shared, and is warm, connected, and friendly.

Passive Constructive Response
Person B looks up from their phone but doesn't put it away. Then they say, "Wow, really? Nice. Did you win any money or anything?" and looks briefly back at the phone screen.

This response is not bad, per se, but it is low energy and may be delayed, weak, or distracted, making the speaker feel unimportant or unacknowledged. It's like throwing a damp towel over things.

Active Destructive Response

Person B gets up, puts their phone away, and frowns, saying, "What, you don't mean to say you actually entered that lame competition? Ouch, be careful, you don't want to be associated with such an amateur organization..."

This response is actively and deliberately going against the spirit of the message being shared and is dismissive and demeaning.

Passive Destructive Response

"What's that? Oh, cool. By the way did I tell you what I saw at the grocery store this morning?"

This response is characterized by the listener avoiding or ignoring the speaker and their message, and a hostile refusal to engage in favor of turning the conversation back to themselves.

It won't surprise you to hear that it is only active constructive response types that are associated with relationship satisfaction and feelings of intimacy, trust, and commitment (Gable et al., 2004). If any of the other types of responses are routinely used, things will steadily go in the other direction. The speaker will gradually learn that their message will not be received with any support or enthusiasm, and so they will just stop sharing anything. Over time, this creates feelings of disconnection, alienation, and a loss of intimacy. Trust and closeness will gradually erode.

What's interesting about this model is that it captures a form of poor communication that might otherwise be too subtle to notice. You may have someone in your life who always seems to leave you feeling unimportant or even degraded after every interaction. Why? It may be because they routinely respond in destructive or passive ways every time you open up and share something with them. An unresponsive or even destructive conversation partner can wear away at someone's self-esteem over time.

On the other hand, if anyone has ever told you that "you don't listen" or seems super reluctant to share anything with you, ask yourself honestly if you respond to them in an active and constructive way. They may be reflecting a loss of synchrony in your communication.

Here are some ways that you can start to be a more active and constructive responder:

Respond Empathically

This means centering their emotional experience. Give their unique perception your full attention, and acknowledge it for what it is, regardless of what it means for you or whether you agree or not. Remember that just as communication can be verbal and nonverbal, so can the expression of empathy—use your body language, voice, and facial expression to convey empathy, too. Match their tone of voice, reflect their expression, and mirror their emotional experience. If you're not sure what this would look like, ask yourself *why* they have shared what they have shared with you. Chances are, they want you to acknowledge and affirm their experience.

Show Genuine Interest

You can do this by asking questions, by making positive and supportive comments, or even by giving a few compliments, if that seems appropriate. The important thing, however, is that you really are genuine. People can tell! Fake enthusiasm is arguably worse than genuine neutrality. To that end, avoid giving extreme and over-the-top responses that will only invite suspicion. So, instead of "That's so utterly incredible! I have never heard of anything so impressive in my life!" just say "That is really something. Well done! You must be so pleased!"

If You Can't Be Positive, At Least Be Constructive

You're probably wondering: if you're meant to be genuine *and* positive, what do you do if you sincerely don't care that much? Well, this is where tact comes in. Take a look again at the response above—"That is really something. Well done! You must be so pleased!" This is a kind, thoughtful, and polite positive response, but it is also perfectly appropriate if you just so happen to not care about films or have mixed feelings about the award your friend has won. In other words, you can always be polite and kind even if not explicitly positive, and even if you really can't be positive, at least be constructive.

Remember, it's about them, not you: "Woah, an award! That's unexpected. Tell me everything—will there be some kind of ceremony?" Notice that in this response, you are being constructive because you are deliberately seeking to maintain and support the connection and sense of harmony in the relationship, without strictly needing to agree or be on the same page emotionally.

A few final tips:

- Be careful about sudden topic changes mid-conversation. Even if you don't mean it, suddenly switching can leave the other person feeling abandoned, dismissed, or ignored. Try not to be suddenly distracted by something else going on around you, or abruptly mention something you just thought of before the conversation feels like it has naturally come to a close.
- Occasionally you will encounter passive-aggressive responses from

other people, or things that seem okay on the surface but leave you feeling dismissed. If this happens, don't let it fester—call it out immediately. "Hey, I really do want to hear about what you saw at the supermarket, but I was still talking to you about my award. I'm really excited about it." Sometimes, being direct is enough to clear away possible assumptions and misunderstandings.
- Watch out for subtly invalidating someone's experiences or perceptions of an event. Let's say the person receiving the award is not excited at all; it would be just as destructive to respond with extreme enthusiasm that contradicts theirs, or suggest in some way that their reaction is wrong.

Shift Responses Versus Support Responses

Have you ever spoken to someone who constantly turns the conversation back to themselves? You might mention a vacation you've been on, and they respond by telling you a vacation *they've* been on. You say you've had a bad day, and they tell you they've had a worse one. You begin to share your opinion about something, and they quickly interrupt you, finishing your sentence with their own opinion.

Annoying, right? If you've ever encountered this before, you'll know what "conversational narcissism" is—and just how badly it can damage a sense of connection, understanding, and empathy. This kind of behavior may also be quite subtle. You may not notice it at first, but you find yourself constantly leaving conversations feeling more like an audience member than an equal conversation partner. Conversational narcissism can look on the surface like an ordinary dialogue . . . but it isn't. Instead of a healthy, dynamic to-and-fro, such a conversation is really just a monologue with extra pieces.

Sadly, all of us have the potential to be conversational narcissists. This bad habit is easier to spot in others when you're on the wrong end of the stick, but it's pretty common to fall into this trap yourself without realizing it.

Charles Derber is a sociologist who has researched the dynamics of attention, power dynamics, and focus in conversations, and coined the term "conversational narcissism." He says that no matter how subtle and complex our responses can be, they tend to fall into two broad categories:

1. Shift responses
2. Support responses

Shift responses shift the focus of the conversation back onto you, while support responses maintain the focus on the other person, the speaker. It's basically a question of allowing the focus and content of the dialogue to remain with the other person, or deliberately saying something to steer the focus and content onto yourself. Take this example:

Conversation 1

A: So, little Johnny started second grade today!

B: Oh, gosh, second grade! I can still remember those days like they were yesterday, although Annie was a complete angel at school, so I can't complain.

Conversation 2

A: So, little Johnny started second grade today!

B: Oh, gosh, second grade! How is he feeling about it?

Can you tell which of B's comments above is a shift response, and which is a support response? In Vonversation 1, the focus is on Speaker A and the topic of Johnny going to second grade. Speaker B, however, shifts this focus onto themselves and introduces an anecdote about when their own child went to second grade. In conversation 2, this doesn't happen—Speaker B asks a question that keeps focus on the topic introduced by Speaker A.

Of course, this is a rather subtle example. You could say, "Well, Speaker B is not shifting the conversation anywhere; they're still talking about kids going to second grade. Besides, Speaker B isn't talking about themselves but their child, Annie." However, this is why conversational narcissism can be so difficult to spot. If you read the two conversations again, you'll see that even though it's small, there is a definite shift in the first conversation that isn't present in the second. What's more, a conversational narcissist doesn't literally have to talk about themselves to dominate—any time they are bringing the dialogue back around to themselves (their opinions, perspectives, experiences, etc.), they are deliberately shifting focus.

Now, if you recognize some of yourself in this, don't worry. It doesn't mean you're a narcissist. It's perfectly human to want to connect what others are saying with things we are already familiar with . . . and usually, that means ourselves! The problem is when this tendency takes over and gets in the way of us connecting with the person in front of us. Sometimes, in fact, our desire to come across as kind, smart, and helpful is the very thing that stops us from being so, and we may not recognize that our attempts to listen, help, or give advice are actually unconscious bids to keep the conversational spotlight on ourselves.

Consider this example. Person A is going through a terrible divorce. Person B, their friend, sees their distress and offers to talk. Person B feels like they can help—they start sharing all sorts of stories about how hard it was when they got divorced a few years prior, and what they did that helped, and how bad it felt before it got better. Person B mentions how after being married twenty years, the trauma of a split can be overwhelming.

Person A (big surprise) is not encouraged in the least by this, and eventually snaps, "Okay, fine, you win. You had the worse divorce. Good for you. Can we change the topic?"

Now, Person B may feel surprised at this. Weren't they trying to help? Isn't it good for someone to hear that they aren't alone and that others know how they feel? If Person B is honest with themselves, however, they may have to admit that a small part of them was subtly dominating the conversation. In their attempt to help, they wanted to be the one to speak the most, to tell the story, even to be the wise person whose advice took center stage. Throughout all this, Person B might have missed a crucial fact: Person A could not possibly feel heard, because they didn't have the chance to speak! In trying to help, Person B forgot about Person A's story and forced them to listen to theirs instead. Not very empathetic, right?

The above phenomenon can be especially prominent with people who genuinely believe they are more emotionally intelligent, empathetic, and clued up on the psychological theories of the day. But the content doesn't matter—if such a person is repeatedly shifting the conversation back to themselves, they will be felt to be poor listeners, and communication will break down. You may find yourself inadvertently setting up a subtle battle for attention: You shift to yourself, then the other person, feeling slighted, shifts to themselves . . . fast forward and the conversation has broken down, and there are only two people monologuing in one another's presence!

Try to imagine that a good conversation is like tossing a ball back and forth, or playing tennis. The game only works if there is a true back and forth; everything stops if one person just keeps holding on to the ball. Conversational narcissists are very resistant to tossing the ball over, and the worst damage may be done by the more subtle attempts. For example, we might respond *initially* with an active constructive response, but then immediately follow it with something that brings us back into the limelight:

A: "Since I had Covid, I've been absolutely exhausted all the time."

B: "Oh no, have you? That's tough. Believe me I know—I had Covid *twice* last year and it was hell."

Now, the above exchange is not the end of the world, provided Speaker B gracefully allows Speaker A to have their turn with the ball again, so to speak. However, look what happens if they attempt to snatch it right back again:

A: "Since I had Covid I've been absolutely exhausted all the time."

B: "Oh no, have you? That's tough. Believe me I know—I had Covid *twice* last year and it was hell."

A: "Yeah? I've only had it once, as far as I can tell. But it was pretty bad. I've heard some people take months to get better..."

B: "I didn't. I got better pretty quickly, thankfully. I have a strong immune system."

At this point in the conversation, what option does Speaker A have? They can either engage in a game of one-upmanship to determine who had Covid the worst or the most times, or who got over it the fastest and has the best immune system . . . or they can check out of the conversation entirely. If they continue the conversation, it becomes a tug-of-war rather than a friendly game of tennis.

One study (Dunbar et al., 1997) found that "most social conversation time is devoted to statements about the speaker's own emotional experiences and/or relationships, or those of third parties not present." It's understandable that people try to make sense of others' experiences by referencing them back to their own experiences, but as you can see, it can quickly lead to people getting trapped in their own self-referential bubbles, and communication suffers.

Interestingly, a study from the Max Planck Institute for Human Cognitive and Brain Sciences suggests that our egos can distort our sense of empathy. In one experiment, participants were asked to watch a video of maggots and were able to understand that other people might also find the video disgusting. However, if the participants were asked to watch a video of cute puppies, while being told that others were watching maggots, they tended to underestimate how negative the experience was for them.

What does this tell us? The lead researcher, Dr. Tania Singer, noted, "The participants who were feeling good themselves assessed their partners' negative experiences as less severe than they actually were. In contrast, those who had just had an unpleasant experience assessed their partners' good experience less positively."

What we can conclude is that people tend to interpret other people's experiences through the lens of their own. We use our emotions to help us understand other peoples', i.e., the more happy and content you are, the harder it is to empathize with someone else who may be suffering. On hearing about their suffering, you might be tempted to respond to it all as though it were just a hypothetical scenario, and not so bad. Your encouragement may come across as tone deaf, and you may launch into advice or stories from your own history that do nothing but center you and your own experiences.

So how do you stamp out the bad habit of conversational narcissism in yourself? How do you develop real empathy? Here are some ways to do just that:

Offer More Support Responses than Shift Responses

A shift response is not always a bad thing. Sometimes you want to change the topic or interject with something from your own life and experience. The question is really the *balance* you strike between this type of response and a more supportive one. Shift to yourself, but then be happy to shift back again.

Make sure that you are always offering more support responses than shift responses. As discussed in a previous chapter, acknowledge their courage, ask a question that clarifies the details, say something that shows you care and are listening, or simply offer a response that shows you grasp the gravity of the situation: "Wow! That sounds tough/strange/stressful/interesting." If you're stumped, ask a question. Another good trick: simply show you're paying attention by saying "uh huh" or nodding—it will be appreciated far more than a shift response!

Here's how that may look in practice:

A: "Since I had Covid, I've been absolutely exhausted all the time."

B: "Oh no, really? When did you get Covid?"

A: "More than a year ago, if you can believe it. But I'm *still* coughing. How crazy is that?"

B: "Coughing for a year? Wow, I can't imagine that."

A: "Well, it's gradually improved, but it's taking a long time. It was pretty bad. I've heard some people take months to get better . . ."

B: "I've heard that too. Long Covid, right?"

A: "Exactly. I mean, in a way it's been good to be reminded to slow down and take better care of myself. Did you ever test positive?"

B: "Me? Actually, yes, twice! But it doesn't sound like it was as bad as yours."

Notice anything interesting in the above exchange? After Speaker B supplies three support responses in a row, Speaker A actually shifts the conversation *for them*. So, Speaker B doesn't have to push anything.

At the root of much conversational narcissism is the secret anxiety that we won't be heard unless we forcefully butt in. But unless we deliberately take a step back, we do not give other people the chance to show us conversational courtesy and be genuinely interested in what we have to say. Unless we give up the habit of conversational narcissism, we will prevent genuinely trusting and warm relationships from developing.

Summary:

- Emotional intelligence is also something we do rather than something we are. Thankfully, it can be learned.
- Empathic listening is total, genuine attention to the other person and the message they are trying to convey. Set aside your own ego and perspective and become genuinely curious about someone else's world, listening to understand rather than to respond. Be curious and receptive rather than

reactive, "listening" to verbal and nonverbal signals.
- To respond empathically, acknowledge their courage, ask questions to clarify their message, convey that you care, and check in with how they're feeling.
- Offer responses that are both **active** and **constructive**, rather than passive and destructive, to create trust and connection. Remember that your response to someone's positive expressions is a bigger determinant of the relationship quality than how you treat them when they're unhappy. Show genuine interest in what you're told and match and reflect people's emotional experiences rather than invalidating it.
- Practice offering support responses (which maintain the focus on the speaker) instead of shift responses (which shift the focus of the conversation back onto you) if you want to avoid conversational narcissism. Try not to continually center your own emotional experiences or interpret other people's experiences through the lens of your own. Instead, see conversation as a genuine back and forth and deliberately

set aside yourself to learn more about others.

Chapter 2: Perspective as the Foundation of Empathy

In this chapter, let's go further into the question of empathy and explore exactly *how* we can become more compassionate, understanding people.

Which Perceptual Position Are You In?

Let's begin by asking, what is empathy, anyway?

One dictionary definition says that empathy is **"the ability to share someone else's feelings or experiences by imagining what it would be like to be in that person's situation."**

A key word there is *imagining*. The big idea is that if you can look at something from someone else's point of view, then you can conceive of how they must feel and what they might be thinking. This cannot be done, however, if we do not possess the imagination needed to think outside of our own perceptual limitations and look into someone else's world.

The idea of perceptual positions comes from NLP, or neuro-linguistic programming. It's a framework that not only helps us improve our communication, it can also give us the tools to navigate conflict and work through difficult situations so that you come out on top. In this model, it's possible for a person to look at any interaction through three different lenses, called first, second, and third perceptual positions.

First position is your own viewpoint.

The most natural and obvious position to inhabit, this is the place where you are in touch with and aware of your own thoughts and feelings. However, it can be a limited position, especially if you are unable to ever leave it.

Second position is the other person's viewpoint.

That is, "walking in their shoes." In this position, you are not trying to look at another person's world as you would see it, but as *they* would see it. You try to put yourself into their perception to better understand their thoughts and feelings from the inside, rather than from first position. This is not quite the same as mind reading (or being a so-called "empath"), but it is expanding your field of awareness and perception to include the possibility of a different perspective from your own.

Third position is the neutral, detached observer's viewpoint.

When you occupy this position, you are seeing both yourself and the other person from a third perspective. You can think of this as a bystander or an uninvolved journalist type who is seeing the facts as they are, without any personal investment either way. This broader view also lets you see the interaction as a whole, and perhaps part of a bigger system, and not merely one person's view versus the other's. In looking at this zoomed-out perspective, you may see cause-and-effect relationships that are otherwise hidden.

So, what is the point in knowing about these three different perceptual positions? From the NLP point of view, this framework is about *obtaining additional information.* **Getting to see different aspects on a difficult situation can bring you closer to resolving it or finding creative solutions**. By understanding that perception is not reality, and that other people are inhabiting perceptions that are completely different from yours, you get a 360-degree view on a situation that you might have missed if you insisted on clinging to your own, narrower version of events.

If you or someone else is consistently trapped in their own first position and all the stories and associations that go with it, it's a recipe for the same dynamics to play out again and again. That said, you'd be mistaken for thinking that the third position is the better one, and the first the worst.

Each of the positions has their advantages and disadvantages.

Stay in first position too long and you risk becoming narcissistic, self-absorbed, stuck on your victimhood, focused on narrow issues and ways of looking at problems, stubborn, or unable to find creative solutions.

Stay in second position too long and you risk becoming a martyr or doormat, always thinking of others while sacrificing your own self-knowledge or boundaries.

Stay in third position too long and you risk becoming detached, unemotional, cold, and overly rational—as though you were inhabiting God's perspective and looking down without much empathy.

The real wisdom comes in your ability to skillfully shift between all three.

A real-world example can help us see how perceptual position switching can improve communication and even resolve conflict.

Imagine that there is someone at work that you are developing quite a difficult relationship with. His name is Mike, and although he gets on well with others, you are finding yourself at odds with him more and more. Mike is older than you by two decades, but he is also your subordinate. He has been working for the company for more than seven years, whereas you were hired last quarter.

The problem, as far as you can see it, is that Mike is extremely resistant to taking onboard any feedback you give him. Not only does he seem to ignore what you say, but he actually pushes back against it, causing some embarrassment for you and once or twice holding up team projects. Things came to a head when he insinuated that although you were qualified, you were not actually experienced, and that he felt unable to follow your leadership. The matter has been referred to HR, where you are dismayed to discover that Mike considers you something of a bully.

What on earth has gone wrong?

Let's try to move through all perceptual positions to get a broader view on the situation and seek out any information we might have missed by too firmly occupying our own first position. You take out three sheets of paper, one for each position. On the first, you fully outline your first position and try to carefully unpack your thoughts, feelings, and interpretations of the problem. You realize you're feeling attacked and undermined, and you're confused and hurt that Mike hasn't spoken personally to you but gone to HR. If you're honest, you are also frustrated by his stubbornness and quietly wondering whether his age has made him inflexible.

Once you've fully understood your own position (don't underestimate this step—sometimes we aren't in fact clear on what we think or feel and need to slow down and clarify it for ourselves!), then move to second position. What does Mike think and feel, from his point of view? Mike has worked for the company for a long time and has done well and is well-liked. Then a new manager, whom he doesn't like, comes in, and he probably feels a little threatened. Don't just make this an intellectual exercise—use all your five senses to try to imagine what it would be like to be Mike. Can you see, feel, hear, taste what he does? Try to look at yourself through his eyes. What do you see? Maybe when you do this, you realize you probably do come across as quite arrogant and unwilling to acknowledge his age and experience.

For the third sheet of paper, you zoom out even further and try to see both of you, at work, in this situation. Something shifts into place, and you can suddenly see it more clearly. Mike is insulted to be managed by someone so young, and you are desperate to prove to Mike that you know your stuff and won't be underestimated. You can suddenly see why this combination has been so explosive! You have been attempting to prove yourself by being firm and confident, but this is only perceived by Mike as haughty, unearned arrogance. You've both been caught in a power struggle and a reinforcing loop. It's only in coming far out of either Mike's position or yours that you can see the bigger picture.

To finish, you might come back to your own position again and ask how your own feelings and thoughts have changed.

- What have you learned that you didn't know before?
- What can you find more empathy and understanding for?
- Where exactly is the source of misunderstanding or lack of harmony?
- What new solutions or ways forward does this understanding suggest?
- What information do you still need to understand?
- What false assumptions, biases, and blind spots are you able to let go of?
- How might you like to change the way you communicate with this person moving forward?

After completing this exercise, you realize that the more you double down and insist that Mike obey you, the more resistant he is likely to be. Mike is not a difficult person, per se; he is just coming at things from a very different perspective. Once you understand that perspective, you're better able to talk with him so that he will hear. If you ask yourself, "How would I feel if I were Mike right now? What would I want?" then you are able to see that Mike might be feeling unappreciated or even disrespected (hence the "bully" accusation!).

You would do better to consciously acknowledge his experience and expertise and try out letting him self-direct more than you would younger employees. "Hey, Mike, you were here five years ago when they did the merger, right? Maybe you could compile a quick page summary to get the rest of us in the loop? You probably know what needs to be included, so I'll leave the details to you."

Perspective-Taking—How to Be Mentally Flexible

This capacity to really see into other people's worlds is not a superpower, and it's not as straightforward as being "kind" or polite. Really, **it takes an act of social imagination to temporarily set aside your own frame of reference and entertain another, possibly very different one**. Before empath comes an act of what psychologists call "theory of mind"—the ability to not only understand that others think differently from you, but to observe their behavior, ascribe emotions and thoughts to them, and even imagine what it would actually feel like to inhabit that mental state.

People with strong emotional intelligence are typically perceptive, and they have a heightened awareness of a stream of data that others may ignore. Furthermore, they are aware of themselves *in relation* to others—so the **emotional intelligence behind perspective-taking is really two forms of consciousness at once: self-awareness combined with awareness of the other**.

Often, people who teach about emotional awareness are doing so from an empathy point of view: i.e., if you can understand someone else, you will automatically be kinder to them. But perspective-taking goes much further than this. Expanding your social awareness means you are mentally flexible, more intentional and focused in the way you communicate, and more able to see solutions. Empathy is just a very nice side effect!

Exercises to Flex Your Perspective-Taking Muscles

In the previous section, we used shifting "perceptual positions" to give us a 360-degree view on a tricky work relationship. But you don't have to wait for communication to break down to start learning these skills! Here are a few techniques to fine-tune your ability to consciously switch perspectives (and yes, it's not something that comes for free—we have to practice! If you don't practice, you'll fall back into the default setting, and guess what that is? Conversational narcissism).

The "Step Inside" Exercise

For this you will need some sort of stimulus or object. A good place to start is a photo, piece of art, or movie still that contains a scene with ideally two or more people in it. Ordinarily, we look at others and more or less see them as objects, as not-me, and tend to dismiss their inner realities, and focus, if anything, on their outward behavior. This exercise forces your brain to work a little harder and see into someone else's experience rather than just linger on the superficial surface.

As you look at this picture, ask yourself:

- What can the person in the picture perceive? (Think about all five senses.)
- What might this person know? What are their beliefs, attitudes, or past experiences?
- What could this person care about?
- What do you imagine they want? What are they trying to do, not just in the picture but in life in general?

For example, let's say you find an interesting photo in a magazine—there are two women sitting outside a shop, there's a small dog, and there's a man entering the shop with a curious expression on his face. Just stop and *really look* at this picture. Then, pick one person in the image, for example, one of the women, and ask the above questions.

It's a good idea to start with the basics: think about the literal world this person inhabits—what can they see, smell, hear? Then move on to their inner experience of thoughts and feelings. You might find it helps you really "step inside" to use first person—for example, "I'm relaxing with my friend and wondering who the man walking into the shop is." Try the exercise with portraits, movies, or TV shows, or even when "people watching" in a public place.

Now, there are a few big caveats with this exercise. Imagine you're sixteen years old and looking at an image of a thirty-year-old. You imagine that they think, "Oh no, I'm absolutely ancient and decrepit! I'm a very boring and uptight person. I wonder which young people I'm going to criticize next!"

You can see the problem, right? The skill you are developing is to look at people from within those people themselves—not look at them from outside, from your point of view. If you fail to do this, you risk merely amplifying and entrenching stubborn prejudices and narrowing your perspective, not expanding it.

The "Step In, Step Out, Step Back" Exercise

Of course, if you were one hundred percent successful in inhabiting someone else's point of view, you'd still be severely limited in your perspective since you'd only be adopting their limits and blind spots. The following exercise helps you practice the *flexibility* needed to switch perspectives in the same way you'd switch lenses on a microscope.

Begin in the same way as the previous exercise and dig deep into another person's point of view. That's the "step in" part. Next, "step out" again by returning to your own perspective and asking: what would you like to better understand about this person's perspective? What questions do you have?

Finally, the "step back" part is taking some further distance from both your own perspective and theirs. This entails looking at yourself looking at them, essentially. What do you notice about how your perspective is influencing the way you see their perspective? What changes when you zoom right out?

For example, let's say you're the sixteen-year-old who steps in, but then also steps out and steps back. You ask things like, "Is there something about being a sixteen-year-old that might be affecting the way I'm able to think about being thirty years old? What would it be like to be a sixteen-year-old thinking about someone older than me? What would the thirty-year-old say about my interpretation of their experience?" You might notice that what you thought was "stepping in" really wasn't, since you were only answering the questions much as you would from your own perspective! Seeing this, you may decide to step in once more and try again.

The "Context" Exercise

So far, we've been talking about perspective as though it were something rather small that belonged privately to single individuals, a bit like a personality. Of course, each and every one of us is also heavily influenced by our background, our politics and belief systems, and the social and cultural contexts we live in. Meaning is never something the individual creates on their own—they always do it in *conjunction* with the shared mores, assumptions and symbols that make up their world.

So, if we wish to really see into people's perceptions, we have to take all this additional data into account. A fantastic way to do this is to consider historical perspectives or the points of view of people who come from completely different classes, ethnicities, nationalities, religions, time periods, and social groups. If you're a man, for example, can you think of what it would be like to be a woman? This is trickier than it first seems—it's easy to flesh out an idea of *femaleness from a male perspective*, but what might it be like to be a woman from a woman's perspective, and vice versa? What does the world look like to someone who has completely different modes of making meaning? Can you inhabit a completely different worldview and see what that feels like?

Historians can be a great help when it comes to developing this kind of empathy. By reading the life stories of people who lived in very different worlds, we can start to appreciate that someone might construct their life narrative in a completely different way from us. Ask yourself:

- What do they think and *why*?
- What does a certain experience mean to them, in their own words?
- Regardless of how you see a situation, how does their worldview inform how they make sense of it?
- How might all of this be different for the way you are making sense of things?

This last point is especially useful because many of us make an error in assuming that other people have worldviews, whereas we are just living in the world as it is. We imagine that they have beliefs and perspectives, but we are somehow just neutral. A great question to ask is, "How does this other person see me? How would they explain *my* behavior or characterize my worldview?"

All of the above three exercises can be used for situations that you are actively taking part in, as well as scenarios you are viewing from the outside, or hypothetical situations. They can be applied to someone you are trying to communicate with, but you can also use them to help you better understand the dynamics between two other people. By becoming curious about how each person sees and interprets the other, how their respective viewpoints influence their focus, and how each might feel, you may find that you garner insight into group dynamics that seems almost like magic.

Once you become adept at being aware of yourself, aware of others, and aware of all the many different angles one can view a situation with, you will never take for granted that there is such a thing as a default position or an objective opinion. You will instead see patterns of mutual interaction—and if you are aware of these patterns, you can step in and work with them rather than unconsciously being at their mercy.

The Road to Hell . . .

. . . is, as they say, paved with good intentions! Consider the following example.

A famous American psychologist is a renowned expert in the field of post-traumatic stress and has written countless scholarly articles and books. When a devastating tsunami hits an Asian country on the other side of the world, his university department joins up with some local charities, puts together a working group, and sends him and the team over to the Asian country to offer relief and aid. Having endured such incredible hardship and stress, the people must, so the reasoning goes, be suffering from extreme PTSD and will be in dire need of professional mental health treatment.

When they get there, they are quick to set up free one-on-one counseling sessions for people to talk about what they've experienced. The lead psychologist has trained several of his students to offer mindfulness, journaling, art therapy, and person-centered psychotherapy techniques in a bid to support the tsunami victims.

Except it doesn't work. The people sit in the counseling sessions stumped and unsure what the point is. The psychology students find these people are presenting with very few if any of the symptoms of PTSD in the DSM (diagnostic and statistical manual) and seem resistant to whatever help is being offered.

Having read the preceding chapter, however, you can probably guess why: Though well-intentioned, such a program was doomed to fail from the start because it completely failed to consider the perspective of the people it purported to help. A quick cultural analysis might have shown that the preference for talk therapy is a distinctly Western preoccupation; the concept of "mindfulness" (at least, as it is reflected through the twentieth-century American academic lens) seems alien to a culture with very different ideas about what human beings are, how they work, and how they overcome problems.

The counseling team worked hard to answer the question "How can we help?" but hidden in this was the assumption that "help" means the same thing to everyone. They might have asked instead, "What would these people consider to be help? How do they view what has happened to them?" or even, "How might these people view me and my team coming in and offering talk therapy?"

This is why perspective-taking is about so much more than empathy, sympathy, or kindness. Good intentions and wanting to help are simply not enough!

Handling Big Egos—Including Your Own

Before we conclude this chapter, let's take a good look at arguably **one of the biggest obstacles to genuine empathy and emotional intelligence: ego!**

One of the main reasons we're often unable to appreciate another person's point of view is that we are simply too attached to our own. So attached, in fact, that we can almost forget that we share this world with others who are as devoted to their experience as we are to ours.

For obvious reasons, most of us want to be right and we want others to approve of us and like us. We want to feel special and important. We like imagining that we are somehow at the center of things. We don't want others to see our vulnerable or flawed side—or we would prefer to believe that we don't possess these characteristics in the first place.

But deliberately pushing against this all-too-human tendency is essential if we are to become more emotionally intelligent and improve the way we communicate and engage with others. The trick is to step outside of one's own ego and look objectively at the defenses, biases, blind spots, assumptions, and prejudices that it introduces. This is by its nature an uncomfortable thing to do—which is why so few people do it!

To get used to the idea, let's begin with the easier task: recognizing and working around other people's egos.

Managing Egotistical People

First things first: "egotist" and "egoist" actually denote different things. The former refers to someone who is entirely self-interested, whereas the latter usually refers to someone who holds the view that one's own self-interest is the driving force behind all human conduct. Both terms have "ego," the Latin word for "I" as their origin, and both will probably prove quite difficult to deal with in everyday conversation.

Are such people narcissists? Not quite. Clinical psychologist and author of *Don't You Know Who I Am? How to Stay Sane in an Age of Narcissism, Entitlement, and Incivility*, Ramani S. Durvasula says that while narcissists definitely are egotistical, not all egotistical people are narcissists:

"A narcissist is selfish, but they also want affirmation and adoration, are highly sensitive to feedback or criticism, and lack the capability for reciprocal relationships, as well as the ability to self-reflect."

The sad truth is that being a little self-absorbed is a rather common human characteristic. Here are some signs you are dealing with someone who is trapped in their bubbles, and how to work with them.

Sign 1: A tendency to be constantly self-referential

Remember the shift response? For an egotist, this act is viewed as a kind of correction—they see that something in the world is not about them, so they kindly step in to adjust it so it *is*! For an egotist, things are only important when they relate somehow to them. Egotists love to use the word "I" and will have countless creative ways of constantly turning everything back to themselves. They may have an annoying habit of sharing personal stories or opinions in situations where they are not warranted or appropriate. The hidden assumption throughout is that the purpose of the conversation is for them to showcase their unique ego, to garner attention and praise, to control and steer the conversation, or even to dominate.

WHAT TO DO ABOUT IT: Running away screaming is usually not an option, but interestingly, Dr. Durvasula suggests going along with it and abandoning the hope of changing course again. Why? Because you cannot force an egotist to be less egotistical, and if you attempt to do so, you risk getting drawn into a battle of the egos.

Sign 2: Lack of interest for things that don't directly serve their interests

If something cannot be made to relate to the egotist in some way, expect for it to be met with lukewarm faux interest at best, or more typically a completely withdrawal of attention. In a conversation in which the egotist knows little about the topic or cannot volunteer anything from their own life, they may take a back seat, get bored, or be non-committal. As unpleasant as it is to think about, an egotist only really wants to engage with things that benefit them—they may fail entirely to see the point of things that benefit others.

WHAT TO DO ABOUT IT: As annoying as it is, Durvasula again suggests not trying to force it! There's no point appealing to an egotist's sense of higher good, or pretending that what you're talking about does in fact relate to them. Rather, find ways to ensure that you are never fully depending on their commitment.

Sign 3: An exaggerated view of their own abilities

This is the kind of person who will be tempted to one-up you in conversation. On the one hand, such a person can be very blatant in blowing their own trumpet, but on the other it can be incredibly subtle. For example, you might notice that someone tends to rewrite history and conveniently remember things in a way that paints them in a decidedly flattering light. If confronted with something negative, you may notice a strange preference for twisting things so that they make the egotist look good—even if it's something they've done wrong! Be on the watch for covert one-upmanship, however. This may manifest as someone playing the martyr or doormat ("nobody is as humble as me!") or centering themselves by repeatedly bringing the focus to their victim status.

WHAT TO DO ABOUT IT: An important thing not to do is get defensive. You cannot stop an egotist from viewing themselves in any distorted way they want to, but that doesn't mean you have to buy into it. Be crystal clear in your own mind what your recollection of events is, and don't be bullied out of it. Take everything else with a grain of salt.

Sign 4: No personal accountability

While an egotist will be forever keen to bring the conversation around to themselves, there's one exception: When the conversation is about who is to blame! In that case, it is never their fault, and they will never take ownership of any actions that have had bad consequences.

WHAT TO DO ABOUT IT: Reduce your expectations. Be careful not to expose yourself by depending or relying on an egotist, and don't take promises too seriously. As much as possible, put distance between yourself and an egotist's actions.

Sign 5: Lack of empathy

It's not that egotists can't understand that other people are in pain; rather, they may struggle to see why they specifically should care. This makes them pretty bad at offering support, or it may mean that they use the opportunity to boost their own egos by taking on an esteemed advice-giving role or playing at being a rescuer.

WHAT TO DO ABOUT IT: It's pretty obvious—do not go to an egotist for help, as they will be unable to listen and empathize. Seek out others who can genuinely offer you that support.

Reading through Durvasula's advice, you might be wondering if there really isn't anything else you can do to protect yourself against an egotist. Sadly, no. Egotists do not suddenly change their behavior when its consequences are brought to their attention—in fact, they may simply double down. Instead, your best approach is to minimize contact as far as possible, maintain a strong sense of self, and make sure that you do have some people in your support network to turn to when necessary.

When dealing with other people's narcissism, set boundaries and calmly and neutrally enforce them. Don't get caught up in trying to make witty retorts or back them into a corner—this is just your own ego talking. Avoid them or change the topic. Keep your distance. Be pragmatic and shrewd, and whatever you do, don't bother getting embroiled in complicated theories about why they are the way they are—it's none of your business. Remind yourself of your priorities, stick to the facts, and have the grace to be guided by your own values without needing other people to do the same. This attitude will help you bolster yourself against the feeling of inferiority that self-absorbed people can instill.

However, now that we've seen what egotism looks like from this side, let's consider it from the other side. If you are the one displaying these behaviors, you actually give the other person very little option but to avoid you, minimize engagement, lower their expectations, and politely dodge you in the future. This tells us something important: If you are being a narcissist in conversations, *people will seldom tell you*. They will simply disappear or pull back. All the more reason to be proactive and make sure that you are not making a habit of these bad behaviors.

How Not to Be an Egotist Yourself

Tip 1: Don't think you're immune!

One of the best things you can do to eradicate selfish and self-absorbed behavior in your life is be honest about the potential for it to exist. If you think "Nope, not me," then chances are you have a blind spot. We *all* have the capacity to be a little narcissistic.

Tip 2: Don't get trapped in a "bubble"

These days, it's easier than ever to curate your own reality bubble where you only ever interact with material that you agree with and people who are exactly like you are. This in itself is a form of narcissism—we forget that other worldviews, other people, and other interests exist, and what's more, we get out of practice with learning to engage with this difference when we encounter it.

Have you ever heard the idea that you are an average of the five people you spend the most time with? Well, if you have very few people in your world, or the people you do have are all the same, then what invariably happens is you create a void—and self-absorption can start to fill that void and make you a limited one-dimensional person. This is why it's important to expose yourself to different people, ideas, perspectives, etc. Constantly remind yourself that you are occupying just a small, small corner of the universe!

Tip 3: Work on your self-esteem

It may seem counterintuitive, but the calmer and more secure you are in your own value as a human being, the less you will feel like you have to prove, and the more you can relax and let others shine. Often, conversational narcissism stems from a kind of anxiety that we are not good enough, not seen or heard, not valued. Our dominating the dialogue comes from a sense that we need to fight for attention, to prove ourselves worthier than others, or to constantly convince others to like us.

However, if you can just *relax* in yourself, you will find you are less inclined to always try so hard, and will start to notice interesting things in the conversation other than yourself. A bonus: you may actually come across as more likeable, more poised and self-possessed, even a little mysterious, if you're not seeing conversations as a competition or battleground.

Tip 4: Focus on airtime, not content

Who is speaking the most? Sometimes, we can mistakenly think that we are being humble, accommodating, and empathetic because we are talking about someone else, giving advice, or saying objectively true or helpful things. But as a conversation unfolds, try to forget the content of what each person is saying, and just look at how much time each speaker is taking for themselves. For example, if you are spending ten minutes talking at length about how amazing someone else is... *you're* still talking. It's still about you! Pay attention and instead make sure that every person present is contributing equally.

Tip 5: Pay attention to the word "I"

Have you ever noticed how ready people are to share their opinion, even on things that only a second ago they weren't even aware existed? Conversational narcissism is about constantly making yourself the reference point against which everything is measured. So, someone mentions a current event and they say, "Well, I think..."

It's a small habit, but done often enough, it gives the impression of a person who cannot process the world except through their own narrow filter of interpretation. It can stunt communication and, frankly, become boring, or worse, invite petty arguments when someone feels equally inclined to tell you what *they* think in comparison. Try to notice how often you're saying things like "I feel" and "I think" in a conversation. Can you focus instead on the topic itself, an objective external event, or what others are saying? Can you ask a question rather than make a statement? Of course, it's impossible to avoid stating your opinion eventually, but try to avoid responding to every conversational prompt as an invitation to say whether you agree or not, or state how the topic relates to you specifically. One thing to avoid: starting sentences with "as a." For example, "As a father myself, I think..."

If you can suspend your ego, genuinely listen, and become curious about something—anything—outside of your own limited perception, you will avoid becoming a conversational narcissist!

Summary:

- Empathy is the ability to share someone else's feelings or experiences by imagining what it would be like to be in that person's situation, and being able to occupy their perceptual position/perspective. In NLP's

"perceptual positions" exercise, first position is your own point of view, second position is another person's, and third position concerns the view of you both from a third, neutral observer perspective.
- By switching between these positions, you gain more insight, understanding, and empathy, and find solutions to problems. No position is best, but wisdom comes from being able to skillfully shift between all three.
- Perspective-taking is an act of social imagination where you temporarily set aside your own frame of reference and entertain another, possibly very different one. Self-awareness and awareness of others means we can develop theory of mind and a certain mental flexibility.
- Build this capacity by looking at pictures of people and trying the "step inside" activity, the "step in, step out, and step back" activity, or the "context" exercise. These will help you strengthen your ability to consider the world through other people's eyes.
- One of the biggest obstacles to genuine empathy and emotional intelligence is

ego—our own and others'. When dealing with people who are constantly self-referential, uninterested in things that don't benefit them, lacking in personal accountability and empathy, and have a heightened opinion of themselves, try to avoid getting into a battle of the egos. Lower expectations, stay firm in your boundaries, and maintain distance.
- Watch for narcissism in yourself, too: Don't assume you're immune to self-absorption, work on your self-esteem, and consciously mix with those who don't always confirm your worldview.

Chapter 3: Taking Charge of Your Meta-Language

Many of us are fascinated with the art of "reading body language" and gauging people's secret feelings by looking at, say, the position of their feet or the slight twitch of their left eyebrow. **Before we can become adept at reading other people's nonverbal and often hidden communication, though, we need to thoroughly understand our *own*.**

Mindful Nonverbal Communication

If what we are saying verbally doesn't align with what we are saying nonverbally, we are likely to send a garbled or confused message. Even if the mismatch is slight, our listeners will unconsciously feel the disconnect, and this may result in:

- Our message being "lost in translation"
- People thinking that we are insincere, hard to understand, or concealing something
- Full-on misunderstandings as people respond to one message and not the other ("I thought you meant...")

Imagine that there are always these two conversations—verbal and nonverbal—running parallel to one another in every conversation. Author Nick Morgan describes in his book *Power Cues* how we can deliberately bring the second, nonverbal level out of the shadows and into conscious awareness. When we are mindful of the way we are moving our bodies, using our voices, placing our eye contact, and so on, then we can ensure that the two channels of communication are in sync. Then, we will come across as clear, strong, trustworthy, friendly, and solid.

To dig deeper, let's consider the way that nonverbal communication actually functions in the world. Typically, according to Morgan, it has five distinct roles:

Repetition: By confirming and repeating the verbal message, your nonverbal communication confirms your overall message and makes it appear stronger. Contradict yourself, however, and it's as though you are splitting up the force of your message and making it weak. An easy example: you say no to enforce a boundary, but you say it while cowering and with a slight fearful expression, your voice making the statement into more of a question, more of a request for permission to say no. Your verbal communication says one thing (no), and your nonverbal communication says another (I don't know? Maybe? What do you think?). If you say no in a firm voice paired with firm, assertive body language, that no becomes stronger.

Substitution: You can say something nonverbally *instead of* verbally. You see someone walk down the road in a ridiculous outfit, and you turn to your friend and quickly raise a single eyebrow. That single gesture stands in for a whole world of verbal communication!

Complementing: Related to but a little different from repetition, this is where we send a nonverbal message that adds a little something extra to our verbal communication. For example, we may be breaking bad news in a professional setting, but near the end of the meeting, we give the other person a quick, friendly squeeze on the arm. The verbal message may be, "I regret to inform you . . ." but the nonverbal message adds a little extra: It may not even be possible to put it into words, but the person is saying that beyond the professional setting, they care and are showing some tactile human warmth and encouragement for the situation.

Accenting: This is a little like putting some of your words in a written paragraph in bold or italics—it tells the reader to pay special attention to these details in particular. Accenting body language does the same thing, just with nonverbal communication. Let's say you're really angry about something, and you bash your fist on the table at precisely the word you want to emphasize most. Or maybe you are expressing your gratitude and wonder at something, and you pause and give a little "chef's kiss" at just the point in your narrative that you want to highlight. It's like using nonverbal punctuation!

Drawing on any or all of the above roles of nonverbal communication will help clarify and strengthen your message, so long as it is connected in a real and honest way with what you're saying verbally. We can use any of the above modes of communication on any of these "channels":

- Facial expressions
- Body posture
- Gestures
- Eye contact (or lack of!)
- Touch
- Use of space
- Voice—volume, pitch, articulation, accent, etc.

Think of the example of a woman in a management position who is finding that people seem not to like her and are resistant to her leadership. Why? There could be many reasons, but one of them could be that her verbal and nonverbal messages are in contradiction. She might have genuine authority and a particular rank in the workplace, and her verbal expression is authoritative when making requests and giving feedback. But her nonverbal expression might be weaker and sending a different message. So, she comes across as false, manipulative, or insincere.

Many female bosses and executives find themselves in this position and wonder why people don't take them seriously. One possibility is that they are unconsciously communicating to others "please don't take me too seriously"! Such a woman might find that the solution is to better align her verbal and nonverbal expressions. So, when she is issuing instructions, disciplining others, or setting hard limits, she needs to make sure all parts of her nonverbal expression match this tone. She may mistakenly think that coy smiling, submissive gestures and body language, "uptalk," apologies, and a soft, high-pitched voice will make her seem nice and non-threatening. However, it will only create resistance since it doesn't match what she ultimately wants to convey: "I'm in charge. Listen to me."

How to Master Nonverbal Communication

There are two golden rules for becoming a more in-tune, mindful nonverbal communicator:

1. Get on top of in-the-moment stress
2. Cultivate emotional awareness

First, a big impediment to being conscious and aware of nonverbal communication—yours and other people's—is anxiety. If you are stressed, worried, unhappy, or in any way uncomfortable, your focus immediately shrinks and goes inward. In other words, you automatically stop paying attention to what is going on around you. Even worse, your anxiety may create a filter through which you misinterpret certain stimuli, so what you think you see in others is really a reflection of your own anxiety.

Stress and good communication don't exist together. Anxiety means you may misread others, send mixed messages, or get confused about what other people are communicating to you. One of the best things you can do is learn to better regulate stress (and indeed, all the emotions) in real-time, as you are talking to someone. Awareness starts with self-awareness. Are you speaking rapidly and not breathing? Consciously pause, take a breath, and slow down. Are you feeling overwhelmed and can see your mind racing to give a response, or getting carried away with wondering what the other person is thinking? Stop and reconnect to the moment. Get out of your head.

- What can you see, taste, hear, smell?
- Turn outward and become curious about the other person.
- Take a deep breath, consciously open your body language, and pause.

Learning to regulate stress goes hand in hand with emotional awareness—after all, you have to recognize that you are stressed in the first place if you hope to get on top of it! The great thing is that the more you develop awareness of your own emotional expression, the better you will be able to see it in other people.

The sad truth is that many of us (especially those who spend more time alone or online than we do with real people in the real world) are quite disconnected from our emotions. One of the hidden benefits of social interaction is that we learn to not only better understand others, but *ourselves*. Try to remember that **you can only ever engage with another person's emotional reality to the extent that you can engage with your own.** So, if you find strong emotions or awkward feelings difficult to deal with, you will not be able to engage with them (or even notice them!) in other people. This is why it's often said that our relationships with others are a reflection of the relationship we have with ourselves. Improve the one and you cannot help but improve the other.

So, make the commitment to yourself now that you will take charge of noticing and reducing stress when it pops up, and also that you will take an attitude of nonjudgmental curiosity at emotions, whether they are yours or other peoples'.

<u>Body Language Basics</u>
You might have seen "body language experts" who read photographs of celebrities or politicians and confidently tell you things like, "See the way he's touching her arm? That's a clear sign they hate each other!" The truth is, reading body language is not like verbal language, where one sign or symbol "means" one thing, so if you only know what each thing means, you can peer into the secret world of others.

Rather, **body language must be thought of holistically, dynamically, relatively, and in context.**

Holistically: What is the whole body saying? How does the verbal combine with the nonverbal?
Dynamically: We read not just a single moment or an isolated gesture, but an expression as it actively unfolds over time.
Relatively: What does XYZ mean *for this person*? How does it compare to others? Communication is idiosyncratic, and we

need to measure our observations not against an absolute, but against a baseline.

In context: What is the environment in which this communication is happening? Where in the world? What time period? What is the background circumstance, and what came before?

So, we don't just make a single, time-limited observation in a vacuum and interpret it with no regard to who we are observing, and where, when, how, and why they are communicating that way. Rather, we take a broad view. Forget about looking for this or that nonverbal "clue." Instead:

Look for Inconsistencies

Again, notice any mismatch between verbal and nonverbal expressions. Also notice whether the communication is at odds with prior behavior or somehow doesn't fit with the situation or the general context. Why? Notice changes and transitions. Become curious about why someone suddenly alters their tone of voice or shifts in their seat.

Look for Clusters of Behavior

A single gesture means nothing. Instead, look for patterns and clusters that point in the same direction. Try to characterize things broadly in terms of *open* or *closed*, and in terms of *advancing* or *retreating*. Is the overall body language expansive, taking up a lot of room, and open? Or are most of the gestures about retreating, closing the body, protecting, cowering? Is the body characterized by lots of movement and energy, or is there a stillness? Each observation is like a pixel, but try to zoom out and see the bigger picture that these pixels are forming.

Don't Be Afraid to Trust Your Instincts

Long before the human species evolved verbal communication, they knew one another nonverbally. There are powerful, primitive, and pre-verbal ways that bodies communicate with one another in space, and some of these are instantaneous and completely unconscious to the higher brain. If you get an immediate impression of someone in a conversation, don't dismiss this feeling, even if you can't quite find a more rational explanation for it. Could you be mistaken or just plain old prejudiced? Yes—that's why you consider gut feelings, but you don't make assessments based on them alone.

What to Look At

Eye contact—Where are the eyes going? Is the gaze direct and confident, evasive, quick, or focused elsewhere?

Facial expression—What do you see? How does it change over time? Is it tight or relaxed, masklike, fluid, downcast, or aggressive?

Tone of voice—Think about pitch (how high the voice is), volume (how loud, but also how much speech there is), variability (is it monotone or varied and dynamic?), accent, articulation (smooth and flowing, or filled with fluff and *um* and *uh*), speed, pacing (is it even or jerking around unpredictably), or strained (are they breathing or is the voice constricted or choked?). Try to think of the voice as a part of the body—how is the person using this "limb"? What does it tell you about them and what they're trying to communicate?

Posture and gesture—Is their body relaxed or stiff and unmoving? Is the body leaden and deflated or light and quick? Imagine that bodily tension is the same thing as psychological tension, only manifested physiologically. What does the *location* of the tension tell you?

Touch—Is there any physical contact? When and how does it happen, and how does it fit with the situation? How do you feel about it?

Intensity—Everything you observe will also fall on a scale. Are they ecstatic or merely pleased/content? What are their interest levels—cool and detached or keenly focused on you? Are their reactions over the top or strangely muted for the situation?

It's important not to overthink it—the good news is that you are already a body-language-reading expert; the only challenge is to make sure that you are relaxed and paying enough attention to be aware of what you know!

The Art of Cold Reading

You may be familiar with the term "cold reading" from those who claim to have supernatural or psychic powers, like mediums, clairvoyants, and magicians. The reader is really just using a combination of visual observations, leading questions, and certain conversation techniques to make it seem like they have a special, almost miraculous insight into the person in front of them.

This may seem like an odd topic for a book about emotional intelligence, but it turns out that making others feel like you know more about them than you do is a rather useful trick for everyday conversation! **If you can understand the basic principles of cold reading, then you can create rapport and connection with other people very quickly, not to mention "read" their subtle and nonverbal expressions to rapidly gain insight into their personalities.**

Four Important Cold Reading Principles

The phony medium notices someone in the audience who is extremely overweight and a little disheveled, with a near-empty pack of cigarettes in his pocket. She says, "The spirits are telling me that they want someone present to take better care of themselves." She watches to see any flicker of reaction. When nobody bites, she quickly changes tack, saying, "the spirits also want me to know that someone here needs to love themselves more and accept themselves for who they are." The overweight person very slightly sits up and pays closer attention, and the medium, noticing that it's a man, immediately says, "they're telling me it's a man ... around mid-thirties, maybe his name begins with a J ... or a D?"

Later, the overweight man leaves the session thinking, "Wow, I felt like that message was specifically just for me! How spooky." But really, nothing supernatural has happened. These four elements, however, were all present to give him the feeling that it had:

Observation

The cold reader begins by noticing all those little things that, taken together, paint a picture of the person. She sees an overweight man who hasn't taken much effort with his appearance, who also looks to be a smoker. She puts all these observations together and makes a guess that this is someone who isn't great on self-care.

Redirection

As it happens, the cold reader is actually wrong in her appraisal, and she gets no response to this observation. But that doesn't matter! She quickly moves on to give the impression that she hasn't made a mistake at all. She says the spirits have "also" told her an additional piece of information, which is cleverly worded to conceal the fact that it's quite different from her first assertion. She switches tack and starts talking about self-love. Notice how the medium suggests the man's name begins with a J or a D—very common letters for male names. Notice also that by presenting both options as one "guess," if his name really does begin with one or the other, she conceals the fact that the other letter was still wrong.

Collaboration

The cold reader deliberately chooses to call on the person in the audience who is actually showing signs of responding to her. Skeptics and deliberately uncooperative people are going to be harder to work with, but someone who believes, someone who unconsciously *wants* the cold reader to be accurate, is going to enter into an unspoken arrangement with them to help them be right. The man in our example may be very invested in being told by others that he needs to love himself more, and is willing to go along with this narrative—even forgiving or ignoring any obvious mistakes the cold reader may make!

Conversation

If the cold reader had to simply sit down and make an immediate claim, she'd probably be very, very wrong. Instead, she draws out the back-and-forth conversation, knowing that it's this closely intertwined involvement between reader and subject that gives her something to work with. The more responses/reactions she gets, the more data she gathers and the more accurate her pronouncements seem. Of course, the audience members don't know (or pretend not to know) that they are feeding this information to the reader throughout.

How can the above four principles be applied to ordinary conversations? These techniques work amazingly well when you're meeting someone new or don't know them very well. The trick is to create rapport and connection. If you can do this with someone you've just met, you can create a sense of real warmth and liking within five minutes—and that's a very useful skill to have! Whether you're networking, dating, or trying to survive a big party, getting others to like you is invaluable.

Good cold readers:

1. Keep their focus constantly on the other person
2. Pay close attention to everything—verbal and nonverbal data
3. Look at the bigger picture to piece this data together and make "predictions"
4. Constantly update and move this picture according to feedback they receive
5. Maintain warmth and rapport at all costs

These are all skills that good conversationalists also possess!

Take a look at the following conversation and see if you can spot the redirection, the back-and-forth, the clue-gathering, and so on.

Person A notices that Person B has a tattoo with several initials and dates next to them, and guesses that these are the birthdates of the person's children. They assume that getting a tattoo of such a thing means this person takes their parenting role very seriously. They also notice something else—taking into account the oldest date on the tattoo and looking at how old the person is, they conclude they must have had their first child very young.

A: "You know, I bet you're a very *ride-or-die* kind of person. I'm the same; if I'm loyal to someone, that's it—they can depend on me for life, you know?"
B: "Yeah? That's really cool. So few people are like that these days, though."
A: "Tell me about it. But you can always rely on family."
B: "Exactly! I always say that."

A: "Families are funny sometimes—they have this way of teaching you the lessons you never knew you needed to learn."
B: "Totally!"
A: "Like, sometimes things happen and they seem like the biggest disasters in the world, and they turn out to be the biggest blessings. And sometimes the people you'd least expect can step up to the challenge and prove everyone wrong."
B: "Wow, that's . . . that's uncanny. It's like you can read my mind!"

Person A starts by making observations and putting them together. They see tattoos, love for one's kids, etc., and start to piece things together. People get tattoos for many reasons—why did Person B do it? To mark a special occasion? Why choose tattoos specifically, which are so permanent and publicly visible? Is this a person who wants other people to know how important family is to them? Why would they want that? These questions need never be formulated so precisely, but they will be swirling around Person A's mind.

Person A says things like "Families have a way of teaching you the lessons you never knew you needed to learn" and "Sometimes the people you'd least expect can step up to the challenge and prove everyone wrong" because they have a working hypothesis: that Person B had an unexpected child when very young, but went ahead and did their best, and now loves their family more than anything in the world. Also, the fact that they broadcast this love might speak to a desire to let everyone know that although the child may have been an accident initially, they are proud of them and proud of themselves.

Within a few minutes of conversation, Person B not only feels completely seen and understood, but Person A has also positioned themselves as broadly in agreement with them, creating a strong sense of understanding and rapport. Even if Person A was completely wrong, however, their statements are also general enough that they can just move on if they notice that Person B doesn't quite respond to them. This is what "cold reading" used for good looks like!

Tips for Instant Rapport

Pay Attention to the Details

Even before you're officially having a conversation, notice everything you can and make educated guesses about the person. Form a tentative theory about their personality, their lifestyle, and their motivation. Then, once you're actually talking, continue to make observations but focus on how they are responding to you, to the topic, to questions you ask. Hold that provisional theory in the back of your mind and constantly tweak and refine it.

Be General . . . But Don't Appear to Be So!

Initially, make claims that are so broad in scope that hardly anyone could disagree with them, but which most of us would be tempted to feel apply only to us. "Shotgunning" is a technique in which you send out an idea and see what hits. If you say "I think you're probably a very honest, kind of nerdy, but also dramatic personality," then you might find the other person grabbing just one of these descriptors and running with them . . . conveniently not noticing that the other two don't really apply!

Similarly, so-called Barnum statements (named after famed showman and hoax-buster P. T. Barnum) are very applicable to most humans, but somehow don't feel that way:

"You can sometimes be overwhelmed by too much change in your environment."

"There were times in your past when you struggled immensely."

"Sometimes you feel that other people don't really understand you."

A variation on this is a "rainbow statement," which sneakily includes both logical possibilities, so there really is no choice but to agree with it:

"You're a kind-natured person for the most part, but you can be tough when you need to be, or if you're pushed too far."

This can be combined with redirection and concealing mistakes. For example, if you say "You're a ride-or-die kind of person" and the response is quite negative, you could quickly say "Of course, you don't take it too far."

There are so many truisms and observations that are incredibly general but will be perceived to be more targeted: Everyone likes to think that they are smart, good with people, trustworthy, honest, kind, helpful, have good taste, have good intuition, and are loyal to those who are loyal to them. Everyone likes to think that there is a little something about them that is completely remarkable or even a little strange compared to others! Use this all-too-human feeling to your advantage.

If you're a good cold reader, even being wrong is a data point. For example, if you say to someone "I'm guessing you're a little concerned about money" and they balk at this, you can quickly add "Which is to say, you take care to stay on top of finances, and so you're never caught short." In essence, you do a complete U turn, but the other person scarcely notices it.

Calibrating a Baseline

What does the person in front of you do when they are happy? When they are sad?

What does a "no" signal look like for them? Ask a question you know the answer to and note the response. Ask a question you don't know the answer to and compare the response you get against the baseline you've established.

You can do this over the entire course of a relationship you have with someone, or merely over the duration of a single conversation. For example, let's say you're talking to Person B from the example above, and you notice that every time you talk about cars, vehicles, or motorcycles, they light up, speak more quicky, smile a little, and start gently interrupting you. You conclude that this is what they look like when genuinely excited by a topic.

Later, you invite them out somewhere to do a different activity, and ask if they're interested. They say yes and agree, but you see none of the same excitement—you tentatively conclude that they are not that interested and may be only being polite.

Avoid Emotional Disconnectors and "Word Trash"

Your choice of words says a lot about you. But is it saying what you want it to?

In this chapter we're looking at "word trash" and why you want to eliminate it from your verbal inventory.

What makes a word *trash* is not an aesthetic thing—instead it's about **phrases and words that create distance and act as "emotional disconnectors." Imprecise language can lack specificity in such a way that the other person finds it hard to connect to what you're saying, and this translates to a failure to connect emotionally, too**. Take a look at some examples:

Just

In 2015, former Google executive Ellen Leanse and her colleagues agreed to permanently remove the word *just* from their office and ban it from all communications. They felt that it undermined the speaker's message and conveyed a weak and confusing sense of deference that actually got in the way of understanding. When you overuse "just," you risk making what you say seem unimportant, and it's as though you are pre-determining for the other person how they should react. The alternative? Say what you mean. Instead of, "I just wanted to ask you quickly . . ." say, "I wanted to ask" or even better . . . go straight ahead and ask!

Any Questions? Anything Else?

This is like a bad verbal tic that's carried over from school days, perhaps, when we were taught it was polite to end every presentation or discussion with a little nod to check if there were follow-up queries. It's not the end of the world, but the trouble with such a broad question is that it leaves things too open-ended and creates an ill-defined gap that people usually struggle to fill. "Any" has no limits. Instead, use a word like "some." For example, at the end of your presentation, say, "We have fifteen minutes left, so we have time for some questions." It's a small thing that makes a huge difference. Offering a narrower range of options ironically gives people more to work with and maintains connection.

Honest/Honestly

This one makes sense: If you have to verbally alert people to the fact that you are being honest with them, the opposite effect is actually achieved. The alternative is just to stop saying this and earn a reputation for being trustworthy the usual way.

Amazing/Awesome!

These words have unfortunately been drained of all possible meaning and will be perceived by the other person as little more than overly optimistic filler. If they are used instead of fresh, genuine compliments or feedback, they may come across as insincere and even a little unsophisticated.

Similarly, try to avoid cliches like *nice*, *beautiful*, or *great*. Instead, make the effort to find an appropriate and not overused adjective. Even better, find some specific action to praise and connect it to measurable real-world benefits. For example, "I was so impressed with how you handled that complaint; the way you engaged with that client spared us all a lot of trouble and may have even earned us a loyal customer."

Slay, Killing It, Savage, I'm Dying, or Even Aggressive Terms like Smashing, Thrashing It Out, Etc.

There are two problems with using words like these. The first is that they tend to be niche words that may only be appropriate for very specific social and cultural niches—and it can be very tricky to decide which niches those are. The second is that this kind of "death talk" is actually a subtle but persistent way to decrease warmth and connection to the people we're speaking with. True, you may only mean it metaphorically and barely give it any thought, but the effect remains.

Normalizing even allegorical aggression, violence, or competition can seep in and gradually erode a feeling of harmony, trust, and connection. Watch out for *hate*—I hate to say it, hate to break it to you, etc.—since these somehow convey violence and aggression, but at the same time lack power and volition, i.e., an awful combination.

War metaphors are mindlessly hyperbolic and lazy, and they litter our language. But we can express ourselves perfectly fine without them! Try instead to use more cooperative analogies and metaphors, or simply forego the metaphors entirely.

Should

This tiny word carries a lot of baggage. When we say it, we're usually communicating many complicated layers of regret, disempowerment, guilt, and more. Using it positions us against some grand external law that we are failing to comply with but nevertheless have to, and it immediately drains away a sense of choice or voluntary purpose. "Should" can conceal enormous judgments and shame; it can allow a sense of eternal dissatisfaction to creep in; it can focus your thoughts on moralizing, criticism, and negativity.

Of course, there are some things in life that you or others should do . . . but be mindful of how you're using the word. For example, if you need to cut a conversation short, don't say "I should go," but choose something positive instead. "It's been so good to talk. See you next week?" With this small change you have moved yourself from passive to proactive, negative to positive. Similarly, if you say to someone "You should have remembered," you are placing blame and admonishment. If you instead say "I'm upset you forgot," you get closer to the truth of the problem and leave the other person the option to make amends.

Can We Talk?/We Need to Talk

Doesn't reading the above just make you break out into a cold sweat? Consider instead what it feels like to be told "Can I speak to you?" Much less scary, right? This is because *speak to* is more specific than *talk* (it has a direct object, for one), and so it doesn't create the same feeling of disconnect.

Elizabeth Stokoe is a professor of social interaction at Loughborough University and has discovered that for some scenarios, it's actually more difficult to say no to a request to **speak** than it is a request to **talk**. Talking can feel directionless and can make people who may worry they're in trouble feel attacked. But "speak" carries a lot less of this baggage. This is probably more pronounced when the other person really is in trouble. If this is the case, say "Can I speak to you about something?" rather than "We need to talk."

How Word Choice Reveals Character

Let's go back to basics: what is language for?

Well, it's a tool.

What kind of tool?

A tool that allows us to capture reality in a symbolic representation so we can understand it and share this understanding with other people.

Now, we like to think that the way we do this goes one direction only: We choose which words we want to use depending on our goals, and then communicate accordingly. But actually, the word choices we make unconsciously can reveal so much about us without our knowing it because it hints at the reality we are trying to communicate. The language we use shows other people how we make internal cognitive maps of the world—i.e., it gives useful hints into our worldview, assumptions, biases, blind spots, and unique ways in which we make meaning.

One useful thing to remember is that **although language is a shared system of symbols, the way each of us uses those symbols is completely unique to us. Listen to how somebody speaks and you get a glimpse into the way they think, feel, and understand their world.**

When you look closely at the choices people make in how they use language, it all seems very obvious, and you wonder why you never saw it before! Some studies suggest that extroverts tend to be louder and speak more and with greater speed. Researchers at Amsterdam's VU University asked forty volunteers to look at pictures of different social situations and say out loud what they saw.

Lead researcher Camiel Beukeboom found that extroverts opted for language that was abstract, direct, and "loose," whereas introverts spoke more concretely about things and used more hedging language (i.e., word "softeners" that reduced the impact of their phrasing—for example, "maybe, you know, this could possibly be a good idea, if you know what I mean" versus "this is a good idea"). Extroverts tended to be "riskier" in their expression, more spontaneous, and less specific, whilst introverts are more risk-averse and measured in their responses.

Look at the differences:

Extrovert: I'm starved, let's get lunch.

Introvert: What do we think—shall we have something to eat? Perhaps a quick snack, I don't know.

Extrovert: Oh, but I could cook for us!

Introvert: Shall I maybe make us a sandwich?

Extrovert: This meal is absolutely sublime! You're a master.

Introvert: This is very tasty. I especially like the tomatoes.

There are other, possibly less obvious findings, too. For example, when it comes to the Big Five personality traits:

- Those who are more open to new experiences tend to use words pertaining to the senses more often ("We're so close I can almost *taste* it" or "I hear you").

- Open-mindedness and agreeableness are also related to more creative verbal expression and more overall "pro-social" language (Kufner et al., 2010).
- Those who show higher neuroticism tend to speak plainly about emotional angst and anxiety, such as "I'm utterly devastated" (remember "death talk"?).
- Those who are more conscientious tend to use words pertaining to achievement, work, harmony, and cohesion ("We'll work something out").
- Jacob Hirsh and Jordan Peterson from the University of Toronto found that extroverts tended to make greater use of words referring to relationships (probably because their internal map of reality is a predominantly social one).
- When many introverts are in a group, they tend to default to problem-solving talk, whereas an extrovert-heavy group will gravitate toward more "pleasure talk" and have a wider range of topics.

Social psychologist James W. Pennebaker at the University of Texas at Austin says that people tend to choose certain words according to what they think is most important. If they are deliberately trying to present themselves in a particular way, however, they will naturally choose words they believe will help them achieve this, muddying the waters somewhat. Pennebaker found that people tend to do all this, however, where nouns and verbs are concerned, but exert less control over their articles and pronouns. In other words, listening closely to articles and pronouns (and other words he calls "functional words") may get you closer to the unmanipulated, even unconscious truth.

Pennebaker and his colleagues developed a software program called the Linguistic Inquiry and Word Count to analyze speech characteristics to look for meaningful patterns. It compared the personalities of those who mentioned more happy versus sad emotions, more "I" than "me" or "us," more direct or abstract, more focused on causal connections or human relationships, more rational or more emotional, and so on. The data tended to show that:

- "Higher rates of 'I' words correspond with feelings of insecurity, threat, and defensiveness," according to Pennebaker.
- Words that express counterbalanced thinking ("except," "but," however") are associated with higher cognitive complexity and possibly greater intelligence and trustworthiness.
- Generally speaking, women tend to use more pronouns and refer more frequently to other people. Men are more likely to use articles, prepositions, and "ten-dollar words."
- The older people are, the less they tend to refer to themselves, the more positive overall their speech, and the greater their tendency toward future tense verbs, not past tense ones.
- When they're being honest, people are more likely to use first-person pronouns (that means "I").
- Pennebaker found that famous published poets tended to use "I" more when they were suicidal or

depressed, suggesting an unhealthy self-absorption or even isolation.
- Following a shared trauma, people tended to use "we" more than "I," possibly to underscore a feeling of social cohesion and bonding.

As you can guess, **context matters** in a big way. A conversational narcissist may use as many first-person pronouns as a depressed and anxious person, but for very different reasons, and the effects can be very different too. Linguistic psychologists have long known that a person healing from trauma or illness may write about their experiences in very different ways as they heal and recover. By tracking their pronoun use, overall focus, and choice of language over time, they are actually tracking the changing way these people think of themselves and the world around them. We need to constantly remember that language is a tool, and ask ourselves how the person in front of us is using that tool and *why*.

Now, all this might seem like a lot to remember—how could you possibly analyze someone's speech or writing when there are so many variables? Interestingly, many of those researching this field tend to agree that human beings are already quite good at appraising someone's personality from their verbal expression (yup, they can even tell what you're like over text or email!). To ramp up this superpower, however, it's worth being more conscious about not just *what* people say, but *how* they say it (including what they're not saying).

Let's look at an example. Let's say you have planned a fun three-day hike in the mountains with a group of friends. On the first night, wild animals eat all your supplies and chew up your gear, putting the whole group in a tricky situation. You're all standing around the next morning, staring at the mess, wondering what to do. Here are some of the things people say:

A: "I can't believe this. I just can't. I knew I should have put it up in a tree or something."

B: "I've got a few protein bars on me. With careful rationing, it will take just six or eight hours to hike back to base camp."

C: "We'll be okay, guys."

D: "Haha! This is hilarious. Listen up, B, I want you to know if we have to nominate someone to eat to survive, I'm choosing you."

E: "Maybe you could not make jokes at a time like this?"

Okay, let's take a closer look. Speaker A uses *four* first-person pronouns. The interpretation is clear: They are framing this mini disaster as a thing that's happening mainly to them. What's more, there's two uses of "can't" and a good helping of regret and self-admonishment. You could safely conclude that this person is a little neurotic, probably quite anxious, and feeling very threatened and overwhelmed. This is likely why they're unable to even think of other people in the situation. Think about the subtle differences in the following:

I knew *we* should have put it up in a tree or something.

I knew *someone* should have put it up in a tree or something.

I knew *you all* should have put it up in a tree or something.

Can you see how just small changes in pronoun use tell you a story about how this person sees their own responsibility and agency in the world, and how they understand their place in the group and within humanity as a whole?

Person B says "I've got a few protein bars on me. With careful rationing, it will take just six or eight hours to hike back to base camp." The focus is immediately on a solution, but notice that this person uses pronouns sparingly. It is not stated "If we ration carefully, we can get to base camp in six or eight hours." Instead, the effect is one of cool detachment and pragmatism. Can you see how different it would have been if they had said "I've got a few protein bars on me. I'll share them with you and lead us back to base camp"?

Person C says "We'll be okay, guys." This is a classic conscientious, agreeable, and optimistic way to signal your belief in the group as an entity. This person is not struggling as much as Person A and is clearly showing what kind of world they inhabit: a shared, collective one. Person D's joke is an interesting response. Why did they react this way? What does it mean that they speak directly to Person B and use such a colorful, arresting image to break the tension? Chances are high this is an extremely extroverted person who is focused on enjoying the moment. The drama and humor suggest a robust, even dominant personality who likes risk-taking and is fairly confident in how things will turn out (that, or they're terrified and trying to conceal it—again, context will tell!).

As you're listening to people speak, constantly ask yourself the following questions:

What is this person focusing on? What are they avoiding? What does this tell you about their values and what they consider important?

How do they describe neutral events? Do they take credit for them, blame others, or position things as "just happening"? What does this tell you about their confidence and their feelings of agency and culpability?

How are they positioning the subject and object in their sentences? For example, do they say "I got a speeding fine" or "they caught me speeding"?

How does their choice of language fit in with the rest of their nonverbal communication? Does it emphasize or contradict? What does this tell you about them overall?

How are people using swear words, specialist jargon, and specific cultural markers and accents? For example, if someone subtly switches their accent when talking to someone new, ask why and what they might be communicating about their beliefs and worldview.

What do they repeatedly say? People can signal their priorities by what they tend to say over and over again. Why, for example, might someone keep saying "But then again that's just my humble opinion"? Taken together with several other data points, you might conclude that this person is in fact a conversational narcissist—but likes to conceal it by repeatedly assuring everyone they are actually humble!

Summary:

- Be mindful of your meta-language and make sure that your verbal and nonverbal signals are aligned. Nonverbal communication can repeat, substitute, complement, or accent our verbal communication. If it doesn't, we risk sending mixed messages or lowering trust. Pay attention to messages sent using facial expressions, body posture, gestures, eye contact, touch, use of space, and voice characteristics.
- To build mindful awareness of your nonverbal communication, try to eliminate in-the-moment stress (by breathing, pausing, and connecting with your five senses) and cultivate emotional awareness (including the ability to tolerate and accept emotions as they are).
- When reading body language, think holistically, dynamically, relatively, and in context. Don't rely on single data points, but look for clusters of behavior, inconsistencies with context, and a shift from baseline.
- Use the principles of cold reading to create quick rapport and "read"

nonverbal expressions to gain insight into their personalities. Observe, redirect their attention, collaborate with them, and gather information during back-and-forth conversation. Pay close attention to the details and make constantly updated predictions, maintaining warmth while you redirect from incorrect guesses.
- Finally, avoid emotional disconnect caused by "trash words" such as "just," "honestly," "amazing," "slay it," or "should."
- Listen to how somebody speaks and uses language to gain insight into their mental models of the world. Notice the focus of their speech, their pronoun use, their positioning of subject and object, and how they explain neutral events. Always be curious about what this expression tells you about the person's perspective, beliefs, worldview, and focus.

Chapter 4: Becoming Emotionally Intelligent

In the previous chapters, we looked at ways to be better conversationalists, how to cultivate real empathy and perspective, and how to become more mindful of meta-language—your own and other people's. **Becoming more emotionally intelligent requires that we also have a sophisticated understanding of what emotions actually are, how to read them, how to feel and label our own experiences, and how to validate them in the people around us.**

Many people mistakenly think they are emotionally skilled when they are really just emotional! However, having emotions and developing emotional mastery are two very different things. It's a little like the difference between every human possessing a heart that can pump blood, whereas only a few humans are trained cardiologists who understand exactly how that heart works and how to fix it when it goes wrong! In other words, emotional intelligence is seldom a skill we automatically possess, but something we need to consciously develop. If we can, however, it can completely supercharge our ability to connect with others and put our communication skills on the next level.

The Emotions Wheel and Learning to Label

Daniel Goleman, the author of *Emotional Intelligence*, claims that so-called EQ is actually a collection of four separate skills:

1. empathy
2. social skills
3. self-awareness
4. self-control

We have looked at empathy and social skills, and now we can consider the third skill, self-awareness, and how to use the Emotion Wheel to strengthen it. The Emotion Wheel is a tool that asks you to dig a little deeper beneath surface experiences, whether they're your own or other people's. It's a way to fine-tune our "emotional literacy" and get a richer and more nuanced understanding of the rich palate of possible emotions.

The Emotion Wheel

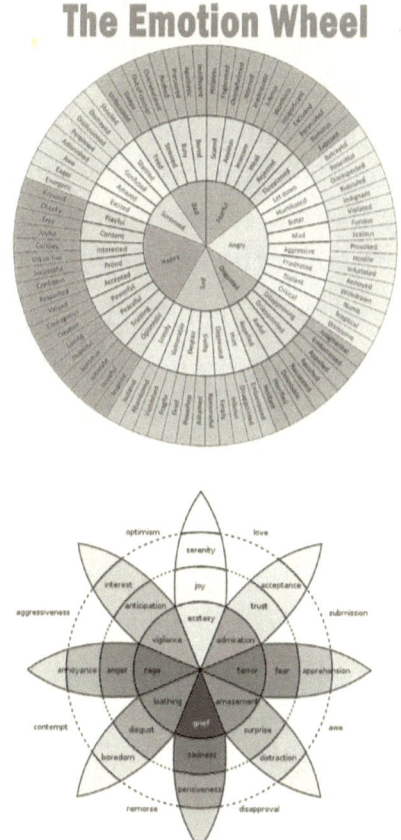

According to Goleman (and many biologists and evolutionary psychologists), there are only a few basic human emotions: sadness, disgust, happiness, anger, surprise, and fear. These experiences are so universal that other animals experience them too, and it's unsurprising, since they relate directly to our survival and speak to our most fundamental experiences of being alive. Think of these emotions like primary colors. There may be a few disagreements about exactly how many there are, but most of us can agree that these cover the bases!

But of course it's not always as simple as this. In the center of the emotion wheel are the primary emotions, but these can vary in intensity. The closer to the center of the wheel, the stronger the emotion, and the further out, the weaker. So, when describing how you feel in an utterly terrifying situation, you might say *horrified*, *frightened* or *scared*. Dialing this emotion down, however, gives us subtler feelings like *anxious*, *rejected*, or *threatened*. Even further out on the wheel and we get subdivisions of these feelings. For example, *rejected* can branch off into *excluded* or *persecuted*.

Different versions of the Emotion Wheel exist, and some of them capture the fact that we can experience a blend of adjacent emotions. Just as the colors on a color-wheel blend into one another seamlessly (and blue-green exists between blue and green), the overlap of, say, *sad*, and *disgusted* might be something like *embarrassed*.

As with all psychological models and frameworks, it's worth remembering that this is just a map of reality, not reality. You may find yourself disagreeing with the way some of the emotion words are characterized, but the idea is to get a systematic hold of more and more nuanced emotional expressions. If you think that there really isn't any difference between, for example, *curious* and *inquisitive*, or think that you could divide the emotion *betrayed* into at least three separate components, then congratulations—you are clearly developing your own sense of emotional discernment!

Use the Emotion Wheel to pinpoint exactly how you (or possibly another person) feels. Since it can be difficult to identify the precise feeling all at once, start with "primary color" and work your way out. Do you feel mainly happy, sad, scared, and so on? Then, move outward on the wheel and see if you can refine the feeling you've chosen a little further. You might start out feeling a vague and ill-defined sense of *anger*, but on closer inspection you realize this is actually a feeling of *humiliation*, which can be further refined to feeling disrespected.

But you don't need to stop there. If you also feel other primary emotions, pick those, too, and identify as many emotion words as you need to in order to capture your current experience. Some Emotion Wheels will be laid out logically so that emotional opposites are positioned opposite one another. If you're really stumped, try to identify what you're not feeling, and work from there!

Now, the Emotion Wheel is not merely an intellectual exercise. Put into practice, it's something that can help you clarify how you feel, which can then improve your communication and help you better understand what you want, what your boundaries are, and how best to communicate them. On the other hand, learning to label feelings means you are quicker to see expressions of emotions in others, which makes you far more likely to understand them and work with them, rather than have that emotion be a source of conflict (we will look at emotional validation in the next section).

1. **Anger**

At work, a fellow employee barges in to take credit for work that you've actually done. Immediately you feel bad, but the negative emotions are so powerful that you can't quite put into words what you're experiencing. You check the wheel to try to get a handle on the experience and build some self-awareness. You are feeling anger, yes, but when you question this anger, you realize it's not the dominant emotion, and that it's milder—closer to, say, annoyance or irritation with the employee's rudeness.

When you dig deeper, you discover that you're actually upset/sad. You follow this emotion and realize that you're feeling hurt and disappointed and as though you are not valued. The initial anger has given way to a deeper, more genuine feeling. Knowing this, you approach your colleague to communicate your grievances in a completely different way than if you had simply gotten angry and yelled at them.

6. **Disgust**

You get back home after a big night out drinking with friends and something feels wrong. You can't put your finger on it, but you just feel . . . bad. Why? You sit down with the Emotion Wheel and can't identify with any of the primary emotions. That's okay, though! You choose the one that matches your feeling the closest—disgust. Moving outward you realize that you're feeling a mild sense of disapproval of your friend's behavior, a little like embarrassment. It's not overwhelming shame or repulsion, but it does make you realize that you need to set up firmer boundaries around your own limits and expectations, especially when it comes to alcohol.

Because you have correctly identified the location of the feeling (you), it means you are less likely to blame your friends unfairly or even to continue on unawares, never quite sure why you feel so uneasy around them.

7. **Fear**

You tell someone that you're afraid about the upcoming exam because you haven't studied enough. But then you stop and question this assessment—is that what is really going on? You consult the Wheel and find that *anxious* and *overwhelmed* are better descriptors of your emotional state. You realize that you actually have been studying a great deal—perhaps too much!—and should probably take a break and work on a little anxiety management.

Because you know this, you change your behavior in intelligent ways—by taking a rest and being kinder to yourself. If you weren't so emotionally intelligent, you might have continued to tell yourself that you were feeling bad because you hadn't studied enough, when in fact the opposite was true. Emotional intelligence always improves relationships—and that includes the relationship we have with ourselves!

8. **Happy**

Let's say you are newly out of an abusive and unhappy relationship, and just starting to date again. It's taking some time to reconnect with what you really feel and what you really want. You meet someone new and though you like them and feel good enough, you don't quite trust your first impressions. Are you happy or just relieved to not be alone? Do you like them or are you enjoying the fact that they like you? The Emotion Wheel can help you tease apart your feelings.

You find yourself gravitating toward words like "accepted" and "content." You realize that the way you are feeling is very gently trusting and relaxed, and that there is a complete absence of drama or anxiety. This helps you adjust your previous misconception about what happiness feels like—i.e., that it is about constantly doubting the other person's interest, always fearful of them leaving, feeling rejected and judged, and so on. The Emotion Wheel can help you fix poor emotional regulation, correct faulty beliefs from past experiences, and help you recalibrate. In the past, you might have broken up with this person because you felt "bored." But after using the Emotions Wheel, you correctly identified this feeling as "safe" and carry on with a person who's right for you.

9. Sadness

You receive a gift from your significant other and it's awful. You immediately express your displeasure; they're confused and offended and soon feelings are running high. You step back from the situation and consult your Emotion Wheel. What happened? While the other person may have focused on your criticism of the gift and chosen to dwell on the feeling of being blamed, you question your own experience and realize that you are just plain sad about it. You see the gift as evidence that they have not put any thought into it, and you feel disappointed they don't know you better. The gift actually makes you feel abandoned.

Now, when you talk to the other person after you've both cooled down, you can keep the focus on this feeling of sadness and not get distracted by the details of the gift, or make them defensive because you're laying blame. This way, you have the greatest chance of resolving the conflict—and maybe even feeling closer afterward.

10. Surprise

Imagine you are the supervisor to a well-functioning and close-knit team, but one day one of the members resigns abruptly, and you find yourself reeling. For a moment, you're not even sure what you think. Other team members are angry and sad, but are you? Looking at the Emotion Wheel allows you to clarify your own feelings so you can properly communicate to the leaving member.

You discover that while you are indeed feeling many different shades of surprise, you are also feeling a lack of clarity and a strong sense of confusion about why they left. You let this insight guide the way you plan to organize your final meeting together. Because you've correctly identified and owned your own emotions, you're relaxed and able to communicate clearly and can plainly articulate any questions you have for them. You clear up your confusion and the matter is resolved gracefully.

11. Bad

Have you ever just felt *bad*? Our emotions are connected to and dependent on our bodies. Sometimes, our feelings are really just messages from our bodies telling us that something is out of balance. Let's say you one day feel "bad" and pause to examine the experience more closely. You realize that this label of bad could more accurately be called "stressed." You've been working too much, eating poorly, and not sleeping. In fact, it's not quite an emotion you're feeling, but simply the sensation of being run down, tired, and a little unhealthy.

Many people who battle mental illness learn this the hard way—sometimes, you are not depressed or angry or doing anything wrong. You just need a nap! This may seem obvious, but how many of us confuse tiredness with boredom? How do we know when we cross over from a productive, flowing state of busyness and into overwhelm? Too many people live lives where their emotional and physiological dysregulation has gone on for so long that they mistake it for their long-term personalities or assume that it tells them something big and serious about their life choices.

For example, someone may feel broadly unhappy at their jobs but not really know *why*, and may conclude that it's too challenging, when the opposite may be true—it's not challenging enough. Or someone might come to believe that they are sensitive and difficult people by nature, when really what is happening is that they are repeatedly having their boundaries violated. They have been ignoring and mislabeling their feelings of anger and indignation as fussiness or inflexibility. **If you become an expert at knowing exactly how you feel, however, you are never in the position of misunderstanding yourself** or setting up miscommunication between your conscious mind and your own needs and limits.

The Power of Emotional Validation

As you can imagine, the more emotionally literate you become with your own experience, the better you will understand the experiences of those around you. It can take a lifetime to learn how to not just identify and name your own feelings, but do the same for others and *keep them clear and distinct from one another.* If we're honest, a lot of behavior we call "empathetic" is really just poor boundaries between our feelings and other people's.

Once you feel like you've had practice naming and labeling your own emotions, the next step becomes obvious: projecting this outward and better understanding other people. With the ability to recognize and name emotions, you can show others that you have heard, understood, and paid attention to their experience . . . not to mention you're in a far better position to help! A great way to get closer to someone is to simply **pay attention, listen, observe what you see, and then (tentatively!) call out the emotion you think they may be experiencing.**

The point of doing so is not to get embroiled in a linguistic exercise or impress people with your therapy skills. Rather, emotional labeling is a way to **validate** someone, which is a powerful form of empathy that creates a deep feeling of connection. Validation is something that every human being needs and craves, and so much of our communication depends on us feeling that we are validated. Sadly, though, many of us feel consistently under-validated in daily conversation.

But what does validation actually mean? When something is valid, it is legitimate. It is real. When we validate someone or their experience, we are not necessarily agreeing with them, but we are communicating that, on some very fundamental level, they have a right to that experience, and that in its own way it makes sense. We are recognizing that what they are expressing is valid, which goes beyond judgments of right or wrong. To witness someone else's experience is really the core of communication—we wouldn't speak unless we wanted other people to really "get" what we were trying to say, right? That's what validation is: the message that says "Yes, I see you. I hear you. That makes sense. I get it."

When you correctly put a label on someone's experience, it can feel extremely validating to them because it means a few things:

- You've paid attention
- You've listened
- You've understood
- You haven't injected any of your own biases or interpretations

All of the above are really ways of saying "*You* matter, and what you are saying matters." It is about the worth of the speaker and their message. In fact, we can validate other people when they are not able to validate themselves—and this can be a big part of healing. How much more valuable it is for someone to help you understand what you *are* experiencing, than give advice or make judgments about what you *should* be experiencing.

Again, validation has nothing to do with agreement or being in the same situation. It's not praise or flattery. Rather, it's about showing someone that you've *received* them and their message, and that it deserves to be heard. Without validation, people feel invisible, worthless, irrelevant, or just plain bad. Worse than disagreeing with someone is ignoring them—because it sends the message that their experience is not even worth consideration in the first place. If you've ever talked to a conversational narcissist who simply could not listen to you or care about what you were saying, you'll know how painful and disorienting it can be—the reason is because you were being invalidated.

So how do we validate others in conversations? One way is to use emotional labeling.

Step 1: Put a name to the emotion (the Emotion Wheel can help).

Read verbal and nonverbal cues and use what you know about the person and the context to make guesses. That's all they'll be initially—guesses—so be tentative rather than rushing in with a know-it-all diagnosis that might miss the mark and cause offense.

Step 2: Verbalize your observation.

This is an attempt to reflect the other person's experience back to them—that means not adding anything that isn't there or leaving anything out. You can use phrases like:

"It seems like..."

"It sounds to me like..."

"I wonder if you're feeling..."

Here, you want to be cautious and leave plenty of room for them to correct you. In the very beginning, try to phrase this labeling more as a question, and deliberately ask if you've understood. "You seem so scared right now—have I got that right?"

This maintains your attitude as one of care and curiosity, not one where you're trying to push your analysis on them. Don't worry if your first guess is wrong; if you adjust it accordingly, the other person gets to feel your receptivity, and trust and rapport can grow. "Oh, I see. Not quite scared . . . but more like anxious. Do you think you're still feeling anxious about it?"

You might also like to add a few generally validating statements, such as:

"I can see why you feel that way."

"That must be really hard/strange/confusing/etc."
"I hear you."
"How frustrating!/How sad/etc."
"I can see where you're coming from."
"That makes sense."
"I'm here for you."

Step 3: Acknowledge the course of the emotion

What triggered it? Depending on the context and situation, this might be obvious, or you may need to ask deliberately what their interpretation of cause and effect is. You don't want to make this seem like an interrogation or forensic investigation, and you don't want to come across as looking to assign blame. Sometimes, it's enough to merely repeat what you've been told but make a few efforts to arrange that data so that it's clear what the source of the problem is.

For example, if the person has given you a long list of unreasonable demands made on them at work, and expressed how unhappy they are currently feeling, you can put two and two together even if they haven't explicitly done so. You can offer a kind of summarizing statement that synthesizes what you've been told: "It seems like your job is causing you a lot of trouble at the moment." You haven't added any new information, but you have offered a tentative interpretation of how it all comes together.

It's worth remembering, however, that not all situations really do have a cause, and sometimes the person will be so overwhelmed with emotion that they are not quite ready to identify the source—or perhaps not interested in doing so. Continuing to insist on it might feel like you are attempting to solve their problems, when they really just want to be heard.

Step 4: Validate the emotion

This is the most important step. It's especially important when you are the cause of the emotions, and the emotions are pretty negative! None of us are neutral, objective beings, and we all come with our own expectations, biases, and assumptions. Validating what we are told is not about pretending we don't have these expectations, but rather about setting them aside and communicating that we accept what we're told for what it is.

Imagine someone is angry with you because you forgot their birthday. You may genuinely feel like it was an honest mistake and that you didn't intend to cause any hurt. Nevertheless, you can see and validate that they *do* feel hurt. Their reality is that you've hurt them; yours is that you did it by accident and are really sorry. Those are different experiences, but they can exist side by side. So you say, "I can see you're pretty mad right now (observing and labeling). You're upset because I forgot (acknowledge the cause or source of emotion), and you have every right to be (validation). I get it."

You can then follow up with apologies or make amends, but notice how your validating them doesn't depend on your invalidating yourself. You can witness and acknowledge their experience without getting defensive, judging their reaction, or trying to force your own experience. For example, "You're overreacting. I already told you I didn't mean to hurt you" or "Why are you trying to make me feel guilty?"

Validating someone else's emotions takes practice and a mindset shift, but in many ways it's the easier option. Simply remind yourself that you don't have to react to what you're told—just acknowledge and validate it. You don't have to decide what you think, pass judgment, compare their experience to yours, find a theory or explanation to make everything make sense, argue with them, praise them, deny their feelings, or try to fix them. Just listen.

You might be wondering, what if you *really* don't agree with them? What if what they're saying sounds completely crazy? Well, continue to validate them. Remember that you are not trying to position yourself as an arbiter of reality or appraising the objective truth of what they're saying. **You're not validating the factual content of what they're saying, but the emotional content.** If they tell you they're terrified that lizard people are secretly running the world, you don't have to agree with this idea—but you can see their terror and validate all the same. "Wow, that must be so scary for you."

One caveat: saying "I know how you feel" or "I feel the same" can be tricky, so try to avoid this kind of phrasing. Truthfully, we often *don't* know how other people feel, and our knowing is irrelevant anyway. Even if we have experienced an identical situation, our responses and interpretations are always going to be unique to us. What's more, when you say something like "I know what you mean" or "I would have done the same," you are subtly suggesting that your support of the other person rests on you being in agreement with them. This can in fact be a slight shift response (see Chapter 1) where we subtly turn the conversation or frame of reference back to us. In reality, what we think about the other person's experience is not that important.

What Invalidation Looks Like

Let's take a quick look at what not to do. The following statements all fail to reflect and validate the other person's experience:

"It could be worse/at least you have your health/think about everything you have to be grateful for/etc."

Translation: You feel bad but you shouldn't—this is judgment.

"I'm sorry you feel that way."

Translation: The way you feel is weird or inconvenient and somehow not quite true. Be honest, has anyone ever felt seen and heard when someone uttered this empty phrase?

"Don't say that!"

Translation: Your feelings are wrong. You need to feel some other way.

"You're over/underreacting" or "you're overthinking this" or "don't be so sensitive."

Translation: Your feelings are wrong. You need to feel some other way.

"I'm not having this discussion!" or a rapid change of topic.

Translation: Your feelings are not worth talking about.

"You've really upset me/I wish you hadn't told me."

Translation: The most important thing about your feelings is the effect they have on *me*. Because I'm more important.

In everyday life, most invalidation happens not because people are callous or unempathetic, but *because* they're trying to show how much they care. Imagine that someone is telling you that they feel ugly and unlovable. You personally think they're gorgeous and adore them, not to mention you hate seeing them so upset. You end up saying things like "Hey, stop saying that! You're *not* ugly. That's ridiculous." Then you start listing their good attributes because you're trying to be kind and helpful. Your intentions are good . . . but you're still invalidating the way they actually feel and still taking over with your own interpretation. They will see your kindness, but they will ultimately not feel heard.

Invalidation can happen especially when we're in the wrong. It takes an enormous amount of maturity and courage to validate someone's experience of you if it's unflattering! But sometimes that's the only way to get through a tricky conflict. It's a question of balance—where we validate ourselves without it meaning we invalidate others, and vice versa. If a colleague complains that you're rude to them, it's tempting to react to defend yourself, to argue, or to rush in with what you think about them. But try instead to validate *their feeling about how you are*, knowing that it's a separate thing from *how you actually are*. You may never see eye to eye with someone, but you can always acknowledge that how you feel, and how they feel, is nevertheless valid.

High-Quality Questioning

By now we know that asking questions is good—but not all questions are created equal. Have you ever been in a conversation where the other person just bombarded you with one question after another? Think carefully about *why* that situation likely did not leave you feeling heard and empathized with. Chances are, it's because the questions were not targeted, responsive, and appropriate. They were not high-quality questions!

In this chapter we'll look at exactly how to use questions to ramp up a sense of empathy in conversations, rather than come across as a nosy interrogator.

Emotionally intelligent people use questions strategically, as very specific and fine-tuned tools in their mission to create rapport and demonstrate empathy. While it's usually better to ask a question than to make a statement, there is a wrong way to go about it. Knowing what we know about emotions, labeling, and validation, let's take a look at how to do it right.

Anatomy of a Good Question

A good question is focused on understanding, not judgment.

Take a look at these questions:

1. "What would you say was the main reason for sending the kids to daycare?"
2. "So why did you decide not to take care of your own children?"
3. "How have you found the new daycare—is it what you expected?"

You can probably see which question comes laced with judgment! Asking a question that comes from a place of judgment might be deliberate, or it may be completely unconscious. Whichever it is, you can expect the other person to respond defensively. If we're being honest with ourselves, sometimes we ask questions in a loaded way, and it may be an underhanded attempt to communicate what we really feel . . . without appearing to do so. Always ask about the assumptions and beliefs implied in your question. Are these assumptions and beliefs helping or hindering? Question 2 is an extremely low-quality question because it is establishing a frame of reference that deliberately, aggressively places the other person in the wrong—the only reasonable response is for them to push back, and so rapport and connection are instantly damaged. Instead, ask questions that genuinely seek to understand, rather than force someone into a pre-existing model of the universe that you are bringing to the table.

A good quality question is open-ended.

Question 3 above is a better bet for many reasons, particularly because it is open-ended. It makes no assumptions at all about how the other person might answer, and does not rig the playing field in the way it's asked (for example, "Are you finding it a relief to have your days to yourself again?").

Good open-ended questions respect the other person's ability to answer as they see fit, rather than choose from some artificially narrow selection of responses you've offered them. You learn more, and they can take the conversation where they want it to go—you may be pleasantly surprised by what you discover when you let go of the idea that you already know everything!

Low-quality question: "Are you back at the university now?" (Possible answers are yes or no).

Average question: "Are you enjoying the university?" (A little more open; room to elaborate).

High-quality question: "What's your university course like?" (Answer can be literally anything!).

Closed questions (i.e., those that have a single word for an answer) are not wrong, but it's generally better to begin with open-ended ones and work your way to more specificity. Mix it up. Try a few broad, abstract questions and let the topic run free, and then drill down with more targeted, closed questions to find out details of when, where, how, who, etc. The important thing is not to hem in your conversation partner!

High-quality questions actively follow up.

As you're talking to someone, you want them to get the sense that you are listening to what they're saying, remembering it, and consciously synthesizing it all into some bigger picture (and you want them to think this because, well, you're actually doing it!). If you only ask a stream of completely disconnected and unrelated questions, and if you don't even remember the answers to these questions, you're not going to be creating this feeling.

Follow-up questions show people that you're listening actively and with intent. You're not just a passive sounding board, but are processing the meaning of what they're saying. When you ask a question that relates to what you've been told—and especially if it encourages them to think more deeply about the topic—then you are showing a certain respect and consideration for their message.

Imagine a good conversation as a way to "think together." You help the other person articulate their perspective. You ask questions that go somewhere, and offer thoughtful and appropriate responses to what you've already been told. Allow others to think more deeply about what you are asking them, and help them articulate the thinking behind their perspectives. In other words, good questions *mean something*.

They're interactive, and they're a living, logical part of the conversational flow.

If someone is telling you all about their complicated family history and how their great-great-grandparents were struggling immigrants, you might listen closely and ask a thoughtful question, such as "How do you think all of that influences your own sense of identity today?" A far less responsive question would be something unconnected, like "So did they come by boat, then?" This second question is not picking up on the emotional content of what is being shared, and not contributing much to the overall flow of meaning.

High-quality questions use paraphrasing.

One way in which it actually is useful to ask a closed question is if you're paraphrasing what you're told and reflecting the message. By doing so, you show the other person you have heard and *processed* the message. Offering a little summary or conclusion in your own words really shows that you've taken on board what they've said—not just the words themselves, but the meaning behind the words.

So, they might be talking about anxieties they have, and you ask a question about their "worries" or "concerns." The meaning is intact; you're just expressing it with different synonyms. Using a closed question could look like: "So do you think you're most concerned about the budget right now?" or "Seems like you're worried about the money side of things. Have I got that right?" Such questions are not gathering more information so much as acting like a supportive, encouraging response that says "I'm listening. I understand."

High-quality questions are balanced with self-revelation.

No one wants to be the only one sharing information about themselves. It's always more comfortable when everyone in a conversation is equally contributing something of themselves. Your goal should be to balance asking and telling. This creates a feeling of psychological safety and fairness. Often, people will give you a signal when they feel like they've talked about themselves too much and are trying to shift focus onto someone or something else: "Anyway, enough about me . . ." or "What about you?" Respect these signals and don't continue pry. As far as you can, try to match their level of sharing—people will trust you more if they sense that you are not demanding they be emotionally vulnerable when you are unwilling to do the same!

<u>Questions You Should Never Ask</u>

Some questions are big no-nos no matter how tactfully you phrase them.

How's the job hunt going? Do you have a job yet? When are you getting a job? (Or worse, when are you getting a *real* job?)

Instead ask:

"What projects are you working on these days?"
"What's inspiring you at the moment?"
"I'd love to hear more about your work."

It's always easier to talk about people's aspirations, dreams, and passions, and not just what they're doing to earn money. There are too many hot buttons you might accidentally press. If you'd like, avoid work talk entirely and focus on what the person is interested in, their skills, hobbies, achievements, etc.

When are you having kids? Are you having (more) kids? Why aren't you having kids?

Another obvious danger zone, but unfortunately still culturally sanctioned for many of us. The trouble is that you may judge others inadvertently when you don't imagine that they have completely different life circumstances, values, goals, timelines, finances, etc. than you do. Having children is a remarkably common life experience, and so people feel comfortable talking about it—not realizing that *how* people make this life-changing decision is deeply unique and personal. The bottom line is it's not your business. As far as possible, avoid these questions altogether unless the other person brings the topic up themselves. Be careful, too, about your own assumptions creeping in when you make statements, even if they seem obvious and neutral to you. You may risk alienating others if you assume everyone shares the same worldview: "Oh, we had a pregnancy scare last year, which obviously would have been the end of the world—thank God we avoided *that*!"

Have you gained weight? Have you lost weight? How much do you weigh? OR But why don't you eat meat/wheat/peanuts/whatever? Why aren't you eating? Why are you eating that?

The same thing applies to this kind of question. Body image is a minefield, and it's best to avoid it completely. Don't assume that a compliment about weight will always be received in the same way you would receive it. Appearance-based remarks in general can be very divisive, as can comments about food and eating. Diet talk can be an enormous trigger for some, but you don't have to have disordered eating to alienate people who don't share your food philosophies.

If you want to compliment someone, steer clear of physical characteristics (which they usually can't control) and focus on objective actions (which they can) or attributes you already know they're proud of. For example:

"I love how creative you are."
"What a great suggestion you made."
"I really appreciate you volunteering to help. It's made such a difference."

Why aren't you married (yet)? Are you dating/single?

How much judgment and assumption in that little word "yet"! Try not to ask questions that will make people feel they need to explain themselves to you (or worse, apologize for not doing what they supposedly should). These kinds of questions have long been associated with nosy relatives who mean well, but their effect is almost always to create hostility and defensiveness. Instead of quizzing people about their relationship choices, circumstances, timelines, or goals, try to show genuine interest in whatever is actually going on in their lives at that moment.

"I'd love to hear more about the people in your life."
"Have you met any interesting people recently?"
"How did you both meet?"

How much do you earn? How much did you pay for your car/home/whatever? How much debt do you have?

Money is a taboo subject and for good reason. The best way forward is just to ignore it completely. There are almost no situations in life where knowing someone's precise financial situation is necessary. What's more, you need to be careful that your own attitudes, beliefs, and assumptions around work and money don't seep in and create potential awkwardness or discomfort.

If you casually say "Oh, why don't you just get a taxi to the airport?" without awareness of the fact that this could cost someone hundreds of dollars that they can't afford, you'll damage trust and connection and make them feel bad. In the same way, if you're virtuously announcing how little you spend on secondhand goods and subtly shaming anyone who spends a lot on luxury items, you're doing the same thing, only in the other direction. It's better to just avoid mentioning the cost of things at all, or your opinion about what counts as expensive or cheap—you could cause offense without ever knowing it!

Summary:

- Becoming more emotionally intelligent requires understanding of what emotions are, how to read them, how to feel and label our own experiences, and how to validate them in the people around us. We need to develop empathy, social skills, self-awareness, and self-control.
- There are universal basic human emotions, but they express themselves in varying degree, variety, and intensity. A tool like the Emotion Wheel can help you build emotional literacy and pinpoint precise feelings and emotions. Primary

emotions include anger, fear, disgust, happiness, surprise, and just plain "bad." If you become an expert at knowing exactly how you feel, however, you are never in the position of misunderstanding yourself and will be a more effective and coherent person as a result.

- The more emotionally literate we become with our own experiences, the better we can recognize them in others. Pay attention, listen, and then (tentatively) call out the emotion you think someone is experiencing. Verbalize the emotion by putting a name to it, and without judgment or interpretation, validate their experience. Remember that you're not validating the factual content of what they're saying, but the emotional content.
- High-quality questions are targeted, focused on understanding and not judgment, open-ended, and tend to paraphrase and connect to what has already been said. Balance questions with your own self-revelation. Remember what people say and follow up with thoughtful questions that show

that you've truly heard and processed the message.
- Certain questions should always be avoided: those concerning jobs, salaries, financial costs, choices around children, relationship status, weight, diet choices, or physical appearance.

Chapter 5: Own Your Limits

It's probably fair to say that for many of us, the biggest impediment to better communication is a lack of emotional awareness and connection. When we increase our empathy, emotional literacy, and ability to communicate—both verbally and nonverbally—our relationships with others improve.

However, **human beings are complex, and not all problems and conflicts can be solved by simply heaping on more and more empathy and understanding.** The other side of the emotional intelligence coin is knowing what to do when resources are limited, people have conflicting needs and goals, and behavior is not as good as it could be. In this chapter, we'll look at how to master the art of boundaries—setting your own and respecting those of others.

How to Create Healthy Boundaries

First things first: not all boundaries are healthy ones. We may be over- or under-boundaried, or we may be guilty of violating the boundaries of somebody else. If you are too rigid, stubborn, or inflexible in asserting your needs and limits, you limit emotional connection with others and may make things difficult for those around you.

On the other hand, if your boundaries are too loose, ill-defined, or permeable (or you don't have any at all!), then you risk overextending yourself, becoming a doormat, or even opening yourself to abuse, manipulation, and disrespect. The best boundary to have, then, is a balanced one that asserts your needs, defends your limits, and yet also respects and considers the needs and limits of the people around you.

Another thing to remember is that even though a boundary, once set, should be respected, it can change over time. That's because our needs and limits change. All the more reason to have self-knowledge and the ability to communicate clearly with others!

Finding your own sweet spot of assertiveness takes practice and effort, but it can be learned. Knowing who you are, what you want, what you *don't* want, and exactly how to say so is a big part of emotional intelligence. When you can take charge of yourself, own your limits, and clearly and confidently let people know who you are, your self-respect will tend to inspire the respect of others.

How to Set Boundaries

Step 1: Know thyself

The thing about your boundaries is that they're *yours*—nobody can tell you what they are or should be. This means that you have some work to do. There are two possibilities:

First, you could use an uncomfortable or unpleasant current situation to help you identify any areas that need stronger or clearer boundaries. Use the Emotion Wheel above or sit with a journal to help you crystalize what's gone wrong and why. Ask yourself:

- What *exactly* is causing my discomfort? (Be as specific as possible, identifying actual behaviors.)
- Is there any activity, event, or person I'm dreading? Why?
- What happened immediately before I started to feel bad?
- If I could rewind recent events, where would I hit the pause switch to make sure I didn't end up feeling that way again?
- If other people's behaviors and expectations were not part of the picture, what would I choose to do here?

By exploring how you feel and imagining what alternatives would look like, you can begin to shape and form your boundaries. Think in terms of needs but also limits of resources, which can be time, energy, money, and so on. For example, you may notice that you are really dreading a night out with certain family members, and after some reflection realize that you're unhappy about being encouraged to spend far more money than you're comfortable with. You identify the level of spending you'd be happy with and decide that this is your new boundary.

The second way is to not wait until you feel uncomfortable, but take the time to fashion boundaries before they're needed. Follow the same introspection process and ask yourself:

- What tends to drain me and what feeds and inspires me?
- What are my ultimate, non-negotiable values in life?
- What things do I need to feel healthy, supported, heard?
- What am I willing to "spend" in terms of energy, time, money, and so on right now?
- What are my priorities?
- What do I consider my "life rules" to always follow?

By doing the above process, you might come to understand that a big principle you like to follow is to live simply and minimally and focus on people rather than material things. You might realize that you have a strong need for a certain amount of alone time and to prioritize relationships over work, for example. This means that when you are next invited out on an expensive evening with your family, you are prepared to draw a clear line in the sand.

Step 2: Communicate clearly

One of the biggest mistakes you can make is to quietly decide what your boundaries are . . . and then keep them a secret. People are not mind readers! It may sound silly, but don't expect people to know what you need or what your limits are without clearly and directly telling them. Don't assume that things are obvious, because everyone has different ideas about what is reasonable and what isn't.

Again, there are two ways to do this: either in the heat of the moment when you need to assert a boundary, or in a more general way when the boundary is not yet actively in play.

How you share your needs and limits depends on the kind of boundary you have. Most boundaries are to do with what you won't accept, and then to draw limits around resources. For example:

Time: "I'm free this afternoon but have to leave after an hour to make my appointment."

Energy: "That's a bit too much for me to take on at the moment."

Emotional capacity: "I want to be here for you and I'm sorry you're upset, but I can't talk with you every day about this."

Personal space: This one can be nonverbal—for example, you politely but firmly step back if someone is getting too close to you, rather than suffer in silence for fear of appearing rude.

Conversational content: "That's not a topic I'm willing to talk about."

Defending yourself: "I don't find that kind of joke funny."

Possessions: "Please don't rummage through my bag again."

Privacy: "I'd like it if you didn't put that picture of me on social media."

Physical or sexual: "I'm not comfortable doing that" or "Thank you, but one slice of cake is enough for me!"

Personal beliefs: "I acknowledge that you disagree, but I've made up my mind."

Professional: "Please don't use my personal phone number unless it's an absolute emergency."

Financial: "I'm sorry, but that is the limit to what I can donate this month."

Step 3: Follow through

This is the step where things can get tricky. Boundaries are *conditional statements*, i.e., if X happens, then Y will result. For example, if someone lies to you, you will no longer consider them a good friend. That Y part of the conditional may be unspoken, but it's always understood to be there. The problem is, people think that a boundary is a demand on how other people should behave; really, it's a statement about how *you* will behave in certain conditions. You are politely but firmly telling people the conditions you hold for further engagement—the "rules of the game" if they want to continue to play with you!

If you don't understand this, you risk making a boundary that deep down you have no intention of following through on. So you say "If you lie to me again, this friendship is over," but you're only saying it to manipulate, guilt, or shame the other person. Then what will you do when they lie to you again? If you haven't genuinely considered the possibility of ending the friendship as you said you would, you are now in the position of having to break your own word with yourself. This is why people take a dim view of ultimatums and sometimes see boundaries as secret threats—unconsciously, that may be just the way they are used.

But this is not a healthy boundary practice. Asserting and upholding your own boundaries is an act of trust and self-confidence and a sign of self-respect. You should never use your own boundaries to try to control another person's behavior, only to communicate your own limits and needs when it comes to your behavior. So, it is entirely reasonable to assert that we don't work on weekends, but we cannot also demand that our employers keep us on if they happen to want staff who are available twenty-four-seven.

How do you follow through on a healthy boundary?

First, think it through and don't say what you don't mean. If you have hard limits, know what the consequences are of those limits being disregarded, and be honest and fully prepared to see them through.

Do not make your boundaries negotiable. If you say you don't work on weekends, but then end up doing a few hours on Sunday evening just to keep people happy, you're sending mixed messages. If people push you, be a broken record and keep politely repeating yourself without changing your message in the least. Be consistent. Remember that someone else finding your boundary a little inconvenient is not a good enough reason for you to drop it immediately or start making concessions. Remember that you are not responsible for how someone else feels about your boundary! After all, there are criminals out there who find it very inconvenient that people try to protect themselves from being preyed upon—but their hurt feelings don't change a thing, do they?

You never need to apologize for setting a boundary, nor should you rush in to try to "make it up" to people to soften your "no." Sure, you can make a counteroffer to do as much as you're willing to, but let this come from you, rather than a guilty sense of obligation. Trying to be polite, we can end up over-explaining or even defending ourselves, which actually weakens our position and invites people to push a little to see how far we'll bend. If you remain firm in your conviction, then others will find your boundaries easier to respect.

If you ever feel like saying no makes you a mean or difficult person, try to remember that having limits is a healthy thing to do and actually creates *more* trust, respect, and connection in relationships. It means that when you say "yes" to something, people value and trust it more. Even better, they learn to see the respect you have for yourself as something that you will extend to them, too—i.e., they will feel more comfortable asserting their own boundaries with you, and a more genuine and honest relationship will follow.

Having good boundaries (i.e., saying no to what you don't want) is really just a way to make room to say yes to the things you do want—and that's something all of us are entitled to do.

Use DEARMAN for Polite Requests and Refusals

In the real world, we are always setting boundaries within the context of other people's needs, limits, desires, goals, and perspectives. When exactly something goes "too far" can sometimes be hard to discern, and there is plenty of grey area between "assertive" and "just plain rude." We want to be polite but also take care of our interests and not be, well, *too* polite!

If striking this balance feels almost impossible, you might try a useful framework that comes from the dialectical behavior therapy (DBT) model that therapists sometimes use with their clients. It's called the DEARMAN acronym, and it can help you stay clear, organized, and mindful during the process of drawing those lines between you and other people. Think of it as a template that can help you say no while still maintaining good rapport and politeness.

If you are in a situation where you find it difficult to say no to the requests of others, or make your own requests, then this can help. Many times, relationship conflict comes down to just this kind of imbalance—either we grow resentment because we acquiesce more than we are happy to, we fail to speak up and say what we really want, or we find ourselves saying no clumsily and causing offense and disconnect.

To avoid all this potential angst, take a deep breath, slow down, and work your way through the DEARMAN acronym:

Describe

The first thing to do is just say what you observe as neutrally and objectively as possible. Stick to the facts and be brief—the goal is to set some background context against which to orient the statement you are about to make.

Example: "A few months ago I agreed to housesit for you and watch your cat while you went away on vacation. I was happy to do this. I also didn't mind helping out when your mom was rushed to the emergency room last month. Now you've asked me to housesit again two more times within as many months."

Express

Next, express how you're feeling using clear "I" statements that do not rope the other person in. Try to help the other person see why your request/refusal matters to you. Naturally, avoid injecting any blame or judgment, or else you risk activating the other person's defenses.

Example: "I feel really overwhelmed with the requests and don't have the time or energy to do it. Because I'm your friend, I do want to help, but I also feel really pressured right now."

Assert

How you feel should then naturally lead to what you want (if making a request) or what you are saying no to (if making a refusal). Don't make any assumptions. The key is to be as specific and as clear as possible and to make clear the connection between your emotional experience and what you are trying to express as a result. Not only does this make you relatable and open a path for others to have empathy, but it makes what you're saying seem reasonable.

Example: "That's why I can't help you with housesitting anymore."

Reinforce

When people hear and respond to a request, show that you appreciate it and say thank you, or acknowledge it in some other way. Relationships are all about reciprocity. People shouldn't respect boundaries or comply with requests in order to get something out of it themselves, but it doesn't hurt to let them know how much it means to you. In the same way, when people respect your limits, acknowledge it. This reinforces and strengthens both those boundaries and the relationship.

Example: If your friend is a little embarrassed but immediately withdraws their request, then you might say, "Thank you so much for understanding, I really appreciate that."

Mindfulness

When you're asserting yourself, stay present and focused. Don't get distracted by things that could weaken your message or confuse matters. Take deep breaths, listen to what you're being told, and take your time. If you feel overwhelmed, take a step back or ask for some time to think. Finally, stay focused on just one request or refusal at a time—if you mix up several different issues in one conversation, you risk emotional overload or confusion.

Example: If your friend is a little touchy and upset about your refusal, you are careful NOT to mention how much you've already helped them out, or how they let you down last year in some unrelated event so they have no right to be upset with you now. Instead, you keep on the specific issue at hand.

Appear Confident

You'll notice this is not *be* confident, but just try to *appear* confident! Even emotionally intelligent and secure people can find it nerve-wracking to ask for something or say no. But if you let your discomfort run wild, it could make you act in ways that undermine your core message. Whether you are saying no or asking for something, try to cultivate a little poise and self-control.

Example: You do a deep breathing exercise before you speak to your friend, and you consciously choose to avoid over-explaining or using softening, hedging language. You calmly and confidently say, "That's why I can't help you with housesitting anymore" instead of "I hate to say it and I'm so sorry, but I think I'm going to have to say not this time—at least, not both times, anyway—if that makes any sense. I'm really, really sorry, though. It's just that things have been a little crazy for me lately, and I'm so stressed, so I hope you understand. Is that okay? Blah, blah, blah . . ."

Negotiate

This is the step where you try to make sure that everyone gets what they want—or close to it. Of course, just asking for something doesn't entitle you to have the request approved—no matter how nicely you ask! Do your best to communicate as clearly as possible, but if someone doesn't hear you or cannot comply, handle it with grace. That means never resorting to making any negative feelings their problem. If they agree, say thank you. If they don't agree, say thank you, too, then decide what that means for the relationship (if anything) and how else you could get your needs met.

If you are turning down someone else's request, it is not unreasonable for them to query this and ask about what you are willing to do, or if there is wiggle room. Decide how much you are willing to compromise, if any, and communicate this clearly and calmly.

Example: Your friend says they understand but ask if there really is any possible way you can come over for just one of the times they've requested. You politely refuse again, but you don't like to see them in a pinch, so you say, "If you like, I can hook you up with a cat-sitter that my friend always recommends? I'll give her a call and see if she's available."

What would the DEARMAN acronym look like when applied to a request rather than a refusal or assertion of a boundary? Take a look at this example:

Describe. "I'd like to talk about how we manage the housework between us. I know we keep things fairly balanced, but for the next two weeks, I'm having to really put in the hours with my thesis."

Express. "I feel completely exhausted at the thought of having to do the housework on top of the thesis, and I am worried about doing well. I've worked hard for this degree, and I don't want anything to jeopardize it at this late stage."

Assert. "I was hoping that you could take on the bulk of the housework for these upcoming two weeks while I finish my thesis."

Reinforce. "I understand it's a big ask, so I thought I might offer to pay you something fair and reasonable to offset the extra effort you'd be making."

Stay mindful. "I know that we've had our disagreements about housework in the past, but today I'd like to just focus on these next two weeks and see what you think."

Appear confident. You maintain friendly eye contact, relaxed and open body posture, and give the other person plenty of time afterward to respond to what you've said. You also make sure you broach the subject when both of you are relaxed and won't be interrupted or distracted.

Negotiate. You work together to identify an amount of money that feels fair, a list of chores to hand over to them, and a fixed start and end date. They can't do a full fourteen days but agree to twelve, and you go along with this.

Alternatively, the other person turns down your request. You respond by thanking them anyway and committing to not making them feel bad for having their own boundaries. It's no big deal. However, if you are in a relationship where you notice that your needs are consistently not met, or that your boundaries are seemingly always pressed on or even violated, you might ask yourself why and be honest about whether it's a good relationship for you.

As you can see, the DEARMAN framework is pretty flexible and can be applied to both the big, difficult conversations but also the everyday niggles that emerge now and then. You can use it to great effect over email, where you can take the time to craft a response that ticks all the boxes. Or, you can use it to help you clarify for yourself your position before you broach a tricky topic with someone. DEARMAN will help you stay focused and on track for the best possible outcome.

Needs, Limits, Requests, Refusals . . . It's a Constant Negotiation

Emotionally mature and intelligent people take responsibility for how they navigate social spaces. They don't let other people take charge of their desires or actions, and they don't wait for it to happen by accident. They know themselves and are secure enough in their own self-worth to confidently seek out what they want and need, but they also know that they share the world with other people, and if they want to form meaningful relationships with those other people, they will sometimes need to accommodate their wants and needs.

Your needs and limits will change over time, and so will your boundaries. Though people don't like to admit it, as social beings we will need to bend at times to accommodate others. This give and take is not a bug but a feature of healthy relationships, and it builds trust and intimacy over time. That's why having good boundaries is not just a single activity you do one afternoon and then forget about forever more. It's something that requires continuous renegotiation—and sometimes you won't get the balance right.

In recent years it has become fashionable to "cut people out of your life" or have strict, ruthlessly strong boundaries that never budge. The truth is, though, as long as we are socially connected to imperfect humans, we will occasionally feel like we're taking too much, giving too much, or not quite understanding one another. This is not a problem so long as we use these occasions to communicate, learn more about one another, and take the opportunity to demonstrate trust and goodwill. In a way, that's all relationships are: a constant shifting and changing of the barrier line between you and another person.

Having good boundaries and the skills to navigate the social world is not about being rigid and inflexible. Rather, it's about being confident in yourself, respectful, quick to forgive, and always ready to learn and adapt as circumstances evolve. Being emotionally intelligent doesn't mean you experience less conflict—it just means you become a lot better at managing and making meaning from it!

The Perfect Apology

Throughout this book we've seen that emotional intelligence almost always goes two ways: As we develop self-awareness, we grow our awareness of others. As we learn to trust and understand our own emotions, we get better at reading those of other people. Similarly, as we refine and assert our own boundaries, we can't help but develop a new appreciation for other people's limits, desires, and needs.

What is the best way to respond to other people's boundaries? Well, if they are reasonable and clearly expressed, then they ought to be respected entirely ("reasonable" here means that someone else's boundary doesn't inadvertently ask you to compromise on your own, doesn't manipulate, and doesn't make "do it or else" threats or demands on your behavior).

Even the most emotionally intelligent of us will occasionally fall foul of someone else's boundaries, though, and sometimes we hurt one another purely by accident. This is where the art of apology becomes a very valuable tool to have in your emotional itinerary.

A Mistake Can Be a Good Thing!

Relationships can be irreparably damaged by a mistake—or they can be stabilized and strengthened. **The difference lies not in the mistakes made, but in how people respond to those mistakes.**

Many of us hate saying sorry for an obvious reason: We hate being wrong. We may feel resistant to the idea that we are the "baddies" in a situation, that we don't always know what we're doing, that we're not perfect, and that our actions have caused harm and upset. However, if we can be mature and conscious enough to own all this, we unlock the potential for deeper, more rewarding relationships.

To understand what a perfect apology looks like, simply start with the shoe on the other foot. Think of a time when someone did you wrong and you desperately wanted them to apologize. What made you feel better? What is the worst way they could have reacted? Probably not apologizing at all, or even worse, trying to shift blame or make you seem unreasonable for being upset. If you ever feel tempted to wriggle out of saying sorry because you think it will make you look bad, try to remind yourself that shirking responsibility often looks far worse . . .

You've probably also felt what it's like to receive a faux apology that lacks any real spirit of remorse. Some of us may even know what it's like to receive an apology that only feels like a further insult! Keep all this in mind when you pitch your own apology. The best ones are invariably those that demonstrate remorse and are sincere, genuine, and voluntary.

It turns out that psychologist Lewicki and colleagues have narrowed down the precise formula for a winning apology, which they believe needs to contain six important elements:

- Expression of regret
- Explanation of what went wrong (without excuses or blame)
- Taking responsibility
- Repentance
- Offering reparations

- Request for forgiveness

Interestingly, Lewicki et al. also list these features in order of their importance—meaning that expressing genuine regret is the most important, and asking outright for forgiveness is the least. That means that if you forget all the elements and rush to begging for forgiveness, your apology is not likely to land well.

Let's take a closer look.

1. Express your genuine regret

It's not enough to simply acknowledge that the other person is unhappy. For whatever reason, human beings want to know that those who have done them wrong also feel unhappy about it—that they experience remorse and regret. The very first thing you need to do is acknowledge the mistake or offense and let the other person know that you're truly sorry.

Have you ever thought what it really means to be sorry? There's a subtle difference between *I'm sorry this situation is happening because it's inconvenient for me* and *I'm sorry that I did something wrong and sincerely regret it because it hurt someone else.* Tone becomes very important here because the person you are apologizing to will be very sensitive to the subtleties in your message, even if you are unconscious of them or think that your real intentions are hidden.

You simply cannot come across as annoyed, insincere, or sarcastic. Saying "I'm sorry *you* got offended" just won't cut it, and the other person will recognize such a statement for what it is: an underhanded act of war! Instead, you need to make sure that you're communicating a real understanding that something has gone wrong, you're to blame, and that this fact troubles you. Send the message that you belong to the same moral universe as the person you've hurt, and let them know that, just like them, you regret your behavior.

Does it matter if your offense came down to genuine malice or was just an accident? No. The harm to the other person is the same, and if you begin your apology by listing all the ways it's not your fault and how you're actually a victim, too, you're just issuing a useless faux apology.

2. Explain what happened

There is a fine line between an explanation and an excuse, and again, tone and phrasing matter. You want to let the other person know how it came to be that the offense was caused... without diminishing the offense or trying to wriggle out of taking responsibility. Share your thinking and reasoning and why certain things happened. Point out the rationalizations behind your choices, especially if you truly did not intend to hurt them.

So much of the offense we feel when wronged by others is because we imagine that someone has deliberately done something to harm us. It can inspire strong feelings of defensiveness against what feels like disrespect and insult. But if you can show that this was not your intention, it can lower that defensiveness a little. You want them to understand that the offense was caused not because you don't care or because you're thoughtless or deliberately trying to create trouble. If it was an error, say so.

If it wasn't an error—well, tread carefully and don't try to pass it off as one. If you've done something wrong because you were reckless, selfish, or inconsiderate, your apology will have more impact if you can acknowledge this fact plainly and then move on.

3. Take responsibility

This should lead neatly to the next step, which is where you explicitly take ownership of the choices you've made and the actions you've taken. Don't assume it's obvious. The other person will want to hear that you take responsibility and accept fault. It's hard to do, but if you can muster enough maturity to show that you're aware you messed up and won't be blaming anyone or anything else, you might find it's actually a relief.

It can be helpful to literally say the words *It's my fault* or *I own up to this. I take responsibility*. Try not to add any ifs, ands, or buts. If you (even subtly) try to suggest that someone else made you do it, or the situation forced you to behave that way, you're not apologizing at all but passing the buck.

4. Repent!

This is a pretty old-fashioned word, but a good one where apologies are concerned. When we feel someone has done us wrong, it's like the whole order of the universe has been upended and thrown off balance. An injustice has occurred, and people will feel negatively until they're able to square away that injustice or make things right again. Repentance is a way to show people we've wronged that we are interested in helping them find this moral equilibrium again. We say to them, "I did something wrong. But you have my word that it will never happen again. Here are some things I've changed to make sure it never happens again..."

The other wants to know that the pain and inconvenience mean something, and that you're not going to do the exact same thing again in a week. They want to know that you've "learned your lesson"! Of course, a promise to atone and do better only has value if you actually follow through. Keep your word and do what you say you will—in this way your mistake can be an invitation into deeper trust with the other person. Be grateful if you have the opportunity to boost your own credibility and strengthen the other person's faith in you—it can make *you* feel that the universe has been put in the right order again, too.

5. Offer to make amends

Connected to promising to never make the same mistake again are any genuine efforts to undo the impact of the mistake you've already made. How are you going to move forward? How can you make things right? It's not always possible to do something to fix or reverse the damage done, but if you can take steps to improve the situation, do so, and do it without being asked. This puts some practical heft to your apology and shows the other person you're willing to take on some of the work of repairing things instead of just letting them clean up the mess.

If appropriate, offer to pay for damages, but if the offense caused is more abstract or emotional, a nice gift of flowers or chocolates can go a long way as a symbolic gesture of compensation. These little tokens don't have to magically solve the problem, but they should cost you something and have incurred some effort on your part to organize.

6. Ask for forgiveness

Only after you've done all of the above can you move on to asking for forgiveness directly. The thing about this final step, however, is that it's optional—and it's there mostly for your benefit, not theirs. If the offense is large enough, you could forego asking for forgiveness entirely, or wait for them to forgive you on their own initiative. If you do ask, however, be mindful of how you phrase things. Express your desire for forgiveness as a hope and a wish, rather than a demand on them. That's because the other person is not in fact obliged to forgive you at all, and even if they are, the offense might be bad enough that they need some time before they're willing to move on.

Think of the request for forgiveness as a formality that you finish off with but deliver without the expectation of being immediately absolved. You simply cannot put the other person in the position of having to relive your guilt or make you feel better when they may still be feeling upset.

So there you have it—structure your apology to tick all these boxes, and you'll give yourself the greatest chance of righting a wrong and maybe even strengthening rapport with the other person. A few things to keep in mind, however:

- Match your apology to the severity of the offense (that is, the other person's perception of the offense, not yours). If you tramped mud over the floor they just washed, it doesn't make sense to write them a full remorse-filled email and send them a dozen roses. That said, realize that your idea of how big the offense is might not match their idea (hint—go with their idea!).

- Express remorse and regret without dwelling too much on how bad you feel. This can be a subtle way of shirking blame, centering yourself, or even passively forcing the other person to pacify you and your bad feelings. Focus on them and their feelings instead.
- If it's a small mistake, apologize as soon as possible. If major upset has been caused, you might want to gain a little distance. Write a formal letter and send it a little while after the other person has time to process. But don't leave it too late!
- If the other person doesn't forgive you or even responds with hostility, accept their reaction with grace and dignity. They may never forgive you, and that's okay. If they're upset, don't keep trying to apologize—speak your mind clearly but just once, and then leave it. There is no need to repeatedly apologize.

To finish off, let's look at what a well-structured apology might look like:

"I'm sorry I yelled at you the other night. It wasn't fair on you, and I can see it really upset you, and I'm sorry (express regret). I lost my temper but not because I don't care about you or wanted to hurt your feelings. I just think I've been so overwhelmed at work lately and have been feeling pretty stressed out (explanation). But that doesn't excuse yelling at you, and I take full responsibility for that. I give you my word I will never do it again. I know it's unacceptable (repentance). If you like, maybe I can take you out for a nice dinner this evening, just you and me? (reparations). I can't go back and change the past, but I hope you can forgive me anyway (request for forgiveness)."

Hard to imagine staying upset after that, right?

Summary:

- Human beings are complex, and not all problems and conflicts can be solved by simply heaping on more and more empathy and understanding. Emotional intelligence means having boundaries that are not too permeable or too rigid.

- Take the time to understand who you are, what you want, and what is unacceptable to you, then take responsibility for communicating that message clearly and directly to others. Whatever type of boundary you are setting a limit for (time, money, emotional energy, etc.), make sure that you are willing to follow through, and not use boundaries to passively control or manipulate others.
- The DEARMAN acronym can help you make requests and refusals while staying polite. It stands for describe, express, assert, reinforce, mindfulness, appear confident, and negotiate. Emotionally mature and intelligent people take responsibility for how they navigate social spaces, and know that their needs and limits are always changing and under constant renegotiation. Real life is messy sometimes; be flexible and open to accommodation.
- Conflict will happen, but what matters is how people respond to their mistakes. A perfect apology can actually strengthen a relationship if it consists of these six parts: expression of regret, explanation of what went wrong (without excuses or

blame), taking responsibility, repentance, offering reparations, and a request for forgiveness, in order of importance.
- Good apologies are sincere and match the severity of the offense. Apologize quickly and remember that you are never owed an apology.

Summary Guide

CHAPTER 1: CULTIVATING CONVERSATIONAL INTELLIGENCE

- Emotional intelligence is also something we do rather than something we are. Thankfully, it can be learned.
- Empathic listening is total, genuine attention to the other person and the message they are trying to convey. Set aside your own ego and perspective and become genuinely curious about someone else's world, listening to understand rather than to respond. Be curious and receptive rather than reactive, "listening" to verbal and nonverbal signals.
- To respond empathically, acknowledge their courage, ask questions to clarify their message, convey that you care, and check in with how they're feeling.
- Offer responses that are both **active** and **constructive**, rather than passive and destructive, to create trust and connection. Remember that your response to someone's positive expressions is a bigger determinant of

the relationship quality than how you treat them when they're unhappy. Show genuine interest in what you're told and match and reflect people's emotional experiences rather than invalidating it.

- Practice offering support responses (which maintain the focus on the speaker) instead of shift responses (which shift the focus of the conversation back onto you) if you want to avoid conversational narcissism. Try not to continually center your own emotional experiences or interpret other people's experiences through the lens of your own. Instead, see conversation as a genuine back and forth and deliberately set aside yourself to learn more about others.

CHAPTER 2: PERSPECTIVE AS THE FOUNDATION OF EMPATHY

- Empathy is the ability to share someone else's feelings or experiences by imagining what it would be like to be in that person's situation, and being able to occupy their perceptual

position/perspective. In NLP's "perceptual positions" exercise, first position is your own point of view, second position is another person's, and third position concerns the view of you both from a third, neutral observer perspective.
- By switching between these positions, you gain more insight, understanding, and empathy, and find solutions to problems. No position is best, but wisdom comes from being able to skillfully shift between all three.
- Perspective-taking is an act of social imagination where you temporarily set aside your own frame of reference and entertain another, possibly very different one. Self-awareness and awareness of others means we can develop theory of mind and a certain mental flexibility.
- Build this capacity by looking at pictures of people and trying the "step inside" activity, the "step in, step out, and step back" activity, or the "context" exercise. These will help you strengthen your ability to consider the world through other people's eyes.

- One of the biggest obstacles to genuine empathy and emotional intelligence is ego—our own and others'. When dealing with people who are constantly self-referential, uninterested in things that don't benefit them, lacking in personal accountability and empathy, and have a heightened opinion of themselves, try to avoid getting into a battle of the egos. Lower expectations, stay firm in your boundaries, and maintain distance.
- Watch for narcissism in yourself, too: Don't assume you're immune to self-absorption, work on your self-esteem, and consciously mix with those who don't always confirm your worldview.

CHAPTER 3: TAKING CHARGE OF YOUR META-LANGUAGE

- Be mindful of your meta-language and make sure that your verbal and nonverbal signals are aligned. Nonverbal communication can repeat, substitute, complement, or accent our verbal communication. If it doesn't, we risk sending mixed messages or lowering

trust. Pay attention to messages sent using facial expressions, body posture, gestures, eye contact, touch, use of space, and voice characteristics.
- To build mindful awareness of your nonverbal communication, try to eliminate in-the-moment stress (by breathing, pausing, and connecting with your five senses) and cultivate emotional awareness (including the ability to tolerate and accept emotions as they are).
- When reading body language, think holistically, dynamically, relatively, and in context. Don't rely on single data points, but look for clusters of behavior, inconsistencies with context, and a shift from baseline.
- Use the principles of cold reading to create quick rapport and "read" nonverbal expressions to gain insight into their personalities. Observe, redirect their attention, collaborate with them, and gather information during back-and-forth conversation. Pay close attention to the details and make constantly updated predictions, maintaining warmth while you redirect from incorrect guesses.

- Finally, avoid emotional disconnect caused by "trash words" such as "just," "honestly," "amazing," "slay it," or "should."
- Listen to how somebody speaks and uses language to gain insight into their mental models of the world. Notice the focus of their speech, their pronoun use, their positioning of subject and object, and how they explain neutral events. Always be curious about what this expression tells you about the person's perspective, beliefs, worldview, and focus.

CHAPTER 4: BECOMING EMOTIONALLY INTELLIGENT

- Becoming more emotionally intelligent requires understanding of what emotions are, how to read them, how to feel and label our own experiences, and how to validate them in the people around us. We need to develop empathy, social skills, self-awareness, and self-control.
- There are universal basic human emotions, but they express themselves in

varying degree, variety, and intensity. A tool like the Emotion Wheel can help you build emotional literacy and pinpoint precise feelings and emotions. Primary emotions include anger, fear, disgust, happiness, surprise, and just plain "bad." If you become an expert at knowing exactly how you feel, however, you are never in the position of misunderstanding yourself and will be a more effective and coherent person as a result.

- The more emotionally literate we become with our own experiences, the better we can recognize them in others. Pay attention, listen, and then (tentatively) call out the emotion you think someone is experiencing. Verbalize the emotion by putting a name to it, and without judgment or interpretation, validate their experience. Remember that you're not validating the factual content of what they're saying, but the emotional content.

- High-quality questions are targeted, focused on understanding and not judgment, open-ended, and tend to paraphrase and connect to what has

already been said. Balance questions with your own self-revelation. Remember what people say and follow up with thoughtful questions that show that you've truly heard and processed the message.
- Certain questions should always be avoided: those concerning jobs, salaries, financial costs, choices around children, relationship status, weight, diet choices, or physical appearance.

CHAPTER 5: OWN YOUR LIMITS

- Human beings are complex, and not all problems and conflicts can be solved by simply heaping on more and more empathy and understanding. Emotional intelligence means having boundaries that are not too permeable or too rigid.
- Take the time to understand who you are, what you want, and what is unacceptable to you, then take responsibility for communicating that message clearly and directly to others. Whatever type of boundary you are setting a limit for (time, money, emotional energy, etc.), make sure that you are willing to follow

through, and not use boundaries to passively control or manipulate others.
- The DEARMAN acronym can help you make requests and refusals while staying polite. It stands for describe, express, assert, reinforce, mindfulness, appear confident, and negotiate. Emotionally mature and intelligent people take responsibility for how they navigate social spaces, and know that their needs and limits are always changing and under constant renegotiation. Real life is messy sometimes; be flexible and open to accommodation.
- Conflict will happen, but what matters is how people respond to their mistakes. A perfect apology can actually strengthen a relationship if it consists of these six parts: expression of regret, explanation of what went wrong (without excuses or blame), taking responsibility, repentance, offering reparations, and a request for forgiveness, in order of importance.
- Good apologies are sincere and match the severity of the offense. Apologize quickly and remember that you are never owed an apology.

www.ingramcontent.com/pod-product-compliance
Lightning Source LLC
Chambersburg PA
CBHW020527080526
44583CB00013B/770